Palgrave Studies in Cyberpsychology

Series Editor
Jens Binder
Nottingham Trent University
Nottingham, UK

Palgrave Studies in Cyberpsychology aims to foster and to chart the scope of research driven by a psychological understanding of the effects of the 'new technology' that is shaping our world after the digital revolution. The series takes an inclusive approach and considers all aspects of human behaviours and experiential states in relation to digital technologies, to the Internet, and to virtual environments. As such, Cyberpsychology reaches out to several neighbouring disciplines, from Human-Computer Interaction to Media and Communication Studies. A core question underpinning the series concerns the actual psychological novelty of new technology. To what extent do we need to expand conventional theories and models to account for cyberpsychological phenomena? At which points is the ubiquitous digitisation of our everyday lives shifting the focus of research questions and research needs? Where do we see implications for our psychological functioning that are likely to outlast short-lived fashions in technology use?

Patrizia A. Ecker

The Digital Reinforcement of Bias and Belief

Understanding the Cognitive and Social Impact of Web-Based Information Processing

Patrizia A. Ecker 🆔
Department of Social Sciences, School of Humanities and Social Sciences
Clinical and Health Psychology
University of Nicosia
Nicosia, Cyprus

ISSN 2946-2754   ISSN 2946-2762   (electronic)
Palgrave Studies in Cyberpsychology
ISBN 978-3-031-89997-3   ISBN 978-3-031-89998-0   (eBook)
https://doi.org/10.1007/978-3-031-89998-0

This Palgrave Macmillan imprint is published by the registered company Springer Nature Switzerland AG.
The registered company address is: Gewerbestrasse 11, 6330 Cham, Switzerland

If disposing of this product, please recycle the paper.

To those who believed in me, inspiring my relentless pursuit of knowledge, and to the community that nurtured my growth as a researcher. This work is dedicated to the dream of a future where technology serves humanity in its truest sense—bridging gaps, fostering understanding, and creating opportunities for all.

Acknowledgements

Writing this book has been an incredible journey, and it would not have been possible without the support, guidance, and inspiration of so many people along the way.

To my family, thank you for your patience, encouragement, and understanding, as I poured my energy into this project.

I am deeply grateful to the mentors, colleagues, and peers who have inspired and challenged me throughout my career. Their insights and expertise have profoundly shaped my thinking and work.

To the friends who stood by me, cheered me on, and offered words of wisdom, your encouragement made all the difference during moments of doubt.

Finally, to you, the reader: thank you for engaging with this work. It is my hope that it sparks meaningful conversations and inspires positive change in how we approach technology and its impact on society.

Competing Interests The author has no conflicts of interest to declare that are relevant to the content of this book.

Competing Interests The author has no competing interests to declare that are relevant to the content of this manuscript.

Contents

Abbreviations

AI	Artificial intelligence
BLM	Black Lives Matter
GDPR	General Data Protection Regulation
HIT	Human Intelligence Task
NLS	Nonlinear least squares
RECRO	Reflection exploration connection reinforcement outreach
SERP	Search engine results page
SMIP	Social media-induced polarization
SPSS	Statistical Package for the Social Sciences
TART	Thinking Absorption Reinforcement Time
X	Formerly known as 'Twitter'

List of Figures

1

Unpacking Confirmation Bias in the Digital Age

Abstract This chapter introduces the concept of confirmation bias, highlighting its critical importance in online information processing. It explores how individuals unconsciously seek out and reinforce information that aligns with their preexisting beliefs, particularly in the digital age. The chapter also examines the feedback loops that contribute to the persistence or moderation of these biases, setting the stage for the research questions and hypotheses that drive the study. Key concepts like the cognitive mechanisms behind news consumption and the social implications of online polarization are covered, framing the study's focus on active content creation and temporal dynamics.

Keywords Confirmation bias • Selective exposure • Digital polarization • Content creation • Artificial intelligence • Artificial intelligence bias • Algorithmic influence • Digital engagement • Temporal dynamics • Conspiracy theory

© The Author(s), under exclusive license to Springer Nature Switzerland AG 2025
P. A. Ecker, *The Digital Reinforcement of Bias and Belief*, Palgrave Studies in Cyberpsychology, https://doi.org/10.1007/978-3-031-89998-0_1

1.1   Overview of Confirmation Bias and Its Significance in Web-Based Information Processing

Confirmation bias, first coined by Wason (1960) and later defined by Nickerson (1998), refers to the tendency to seek and interpret information in ways that align with existing beliefs, thereby reinforcing one's current perspective. This bias is particularly influential in digital environments, where interactions are shaped by selective information exposure, or what Pariser (2011) calls the "filter bubble." In these spaces, individuals are often surrounded by like-minded perspectives, creating "echo chambers" (Quattrociocchi et al., 2016) that continuously strengthen preexisting views. Echo chambers function as digital silos, limiting exposure to diverse opinions and contributing to an increasingly polarized social landscape (Flaxman et al., 2016).

The idea that confirmation bias influences web-based information processing is well supported by prior research. Studies indicate that individuals selectively expose themselves to information that reinforces their beliefs, often subconsciously. As Frost et al. (2015) noted, confirmation bias operates as a cognitive shortcut that aligns with prior convictions, alleviating cognitive dissonance. This bias is compounded online, where algorithms track user behaviour to predict and present content tailored to individual preferences. Thus, the digital space not only accommodates confirmation bias but also amplifies it through design (Knobloch-Westerwick et al., 2020). Research suggests that online environments can reinforce existing beliefs and biases. People tend to prefer information that aligns with their existing attitudes, even when opposing views are readily available (Garrett, 2009; Liao & Fu, 2014. This selective exposure is influenced by factors such as perceived threat and topic involvement (Liao & Fu, 2014). Internet search algorithms can propagate societal biases, particularly gender inequality, creating a cycle of bias reinforcement between society, artificial intelligence (AI), and users (Vlasceanu & Amodio, 2022). In criminal justice settings, AI systems used for bail, sentencing, and recidivism prediction may reinforce existing biases and discrimination (Malek, 2022). While exposure to diverse views can moderate attitudes, high topic involvement and perceived threat can reduce this effect (Liao & Fu, 2014). These findings highlight the complex interplay between individual preferences, societal biases, and technological systems in shaping information exposure and reinforcing existing inequalities.

The evidence suggests that digital communication and technology play crucial roles in reinforcing biases and conspiracy beliefs. Confirmation bias is a key factor, as individuals tend to select information that confirms their preexisting beliefs, which can fuel the spread of misinformation online (Baltezarević et al., 2023). Furthermore, heightened social media engagement, along with partisan trust in government, can strengthen belief in conspiracy theories (Lee et al., 2014). Technology itself has also become a target of conspiracy thinking, with widespread beliefs about popular commercial and public technologies fostering a harmful conspiracy mindset (Trang et al., 2024). The Internet's vast information landscape, which often rewards engaging content over accuracy, offers fertile ground for conspiracy theories to flourish (Cichocka et al., 2016). These factors collectively contribute to the entrenchment of biases and conspiracy beliefs in the digital age, potentially leading to negative consequences such as slowed technology adoption and a breakdown in social collaboration.

Echo chambers and filter bubbles are fundamental concepts for understanding confirmation bias in online settings. Pariser (2011) describes filter bubbles as algorithmically curated spaces where individuals are exposed only to content that reinforces their views. This phenomenon is particularly evident on platforms such as Instagram and Google, where personalization algorithms attempt to predict users' interests on the basis of prior behaviour, leading to a narrowing of perspectives (Bozdag, 2013).

Echo chambers function similarly but with an emphasis on group dynamics. Sunstein (2001) defines an echo chamber as an environment where individuals primarily interact with others who share similar beliefs, leading to an amplification of shared perspectives. Recent studies suggest that the interplay of echo chambers and filter bubbles exacerbates confirmation bias, as users are less likely to encounter dissenting information (Schweiger et al., 2014). By limiting exposure to diverse viewpoints, these digital mechanisms reinforce confirmation bias and contribute to social polarization (Flaxman et al., 2016).

Traditionally, research has portrayed individuals as passive recipients of information (Ross et al., 1975). However, this study takes a more nuanced approach, examining users as active participants who contribute to the selective information cycle through content creation. In contrast to passive consumption, active content creation amplifies confirmation bias by allowing users to share information that aligns with their beliefs. Knobloch-Westerwick et al. (2020) reported that individuals often craft their searches to produce affirming information, thereby intensifying confirmation bias. Schweiger and Cress (2019) also highlight the role of active engagement in strengthening biases, as individuals who create content tend to recall information that supports their views.

This view aligns with the findings of Frost et al. (2015), who emphasize the impact of selective recall on the reinforcement of confirmation bias. When users actively create content—whether through comments, posts, or shares—they reinforce their biases through selective memory, recalling information that aligns with their perspectives and presenting it as fact. This selective information cycle suggests that confirmation bias is not merely a byproduct of passive consumption but also a consequence of active engagement in digital environments.

Temporal dynamics, or the timing of content engagement, plays a significant role in confirmation bias reinforcement. When individuals engage with content immediately after exposure, biases are often intensified. As Knobloch-Westerwick et al. (2020) suggested, immediate recall limits opportunities for critical reflection, reinforcing initial biases. Conversely, delayed engagement can provide moments for cognitive dissonance, allowing users to reconsider their beliefs. Frost et al. (2015) examined how temporal dynamics influence confirmation bias and reported that immediate content creation following exposure often leads to stronger bias reinforcement. In contrast, delayed retrieval can weaken biases, offering a period of reflection that challenges previously held beliefs. This distinction is crucial in understanding the varying impacts of immediate versus delayed content creation on confirmation bias within digital contexts.

The cognitive processes underlying confirmation bias—such as selective recall and interpretive memory—play a central role in web-based information processing. As noted by Ross et al. (1975), once individuals form an impression, they tend to recall information that reinforces that impression, disregarding contradictory evidence. This process is particularly relevant in digital environments, where individuals often revisit and reshare information that aligns with their biases. Bozdag (2013) highlights how this selective recall reinforces biases, as users remember and interpret information in a way that aligns with their preexisting beliefs. Research suggests that belief in conspiracy theories is influenced by cognitive processes such as confirmation bias, intuitive thinking, and jumping to conclusions (JTC) bias. Individuals who exhibit JTC bias and prefer intuitive thinking are more likely to endorse conspiracy theories (Pytlik et al., 2020). Confirmation bias leads people to selectively choose information that supports their preexisting beliefs, particularly in digital communication (Baltezarević et al., 2023). However, understanding the conjunction fallacy and considering disconfirming evidence may help counter conspiracy theory beliefs (Stall & Petrocelli, 2022). Interestingly, some scholars argue that the tendency to reject conspiracy theories without proper evaluation, termed "conspiracy theory phobia," can also be driven by confirmation bias and pragmatic hypothesis testing (Räikkä & Basham, 2018). These findings highlight the complex cognitive processes underlying both belief and disbelief in conspiracy theories, emphasizing the importance of critical thinking and evidence evaluation in addressing this phenomenon.

Furthermore, Schweiger et al. (2014) investigated how individuals unconsciously structure search queries to elicit affirming information. This affirmative search behaviour alleviates cognitive dissonance, allowing individuals to maintain a coherent belief structure. Knobloch-Westerwick et al. (2020) further support this view, observing that confirmation bias is a self-reinforcing mechanism that shapes both information recall and subsequent information searches. These findings underscore the cognitive mechanisms by which confirmation bias persists and intensifies in digital environments, where individuals are continually exposed to information that aligns with their perspectives.

Artificial intelligence (AI) plays a pivotal role in shaping digital environments, particularly in reinforcing confirmation bias through personalized content recommendations. As Bozdag (2013) noted, algorithms often present users with content that aligns with their previous behaviours, reinforcing existing biases. This effect is particularly pronounced on social media platforms, where algorithms prioritize posts, articles, and videos that are likely to engage users on the basis of their prior interactions (Pariser, 2011). AI bias is a critical concern, particularly as AI systems increasingly mediate information in digital spaces. This bias often originates from two primary sources: the data used to train these systems and the users interacting with them. AI models are inherently shaped by the data they are fed, which frequently contains historical biases. For example, Amazon famously halted its AI recruitment tool after it was discovered that the system favoured male candidates over female candidates—a reflection of existing biases in the company's historical hiring data (Dastin, 2018). This case underscores that biased training data can lead AI systems to reinforce and perpetuate discriminatory patterns, even when the bias is unintended.

AI-driven personalization not only reinforces confirmation bias but also deepens filter bubbles and echo chambers. By tailoring content to individual preferences, AI systems create feedback loops that expose users to a narrower range of perspectives, further limiting cognitive diversity. As Schweiger and Cress (2019) observed, this algorithmic narrowing can intensify biases, as users are rarely presented with information that challenges their beliefs. Consequently, AI systems that rely on user preferences risk exacerbating confirmation bias, limiting exposure to diverse viewpoints and stifling opportunities for critical reflection.

The implications of confirmation bias in digital spaces are far-reaching, particularly in the realms of misinformation and social polarization. When individuals consistently engage with content that reinforces their beliefs, they become more resistant to opposing viewpoints (Quattrociocchi et al., 2016). This resistance can lead to social polarization, as individuals within echo chambers grow increasingly entrenched in their perspectives, shielded from alternative information sources.

Misinformation thrives in environments where confirmation bias is prevalent, as users are more likely to accept information that aligns with their views without verification. This selective acceptance of information contributes to the rapid spread of misinformation, as biased individuals share content that aligns with their beliefs, often without critically evaluating its accuracy. Research by Flaxman et al. (2016) indicates that confirmation bias can fuel the dissemination of false information, as individuals are less inclined to challenge content that supports their views. Addressing this issue requires strategies to counteract confirmation bias, such as promoting critical thinking and encouraging exposure to diverse perspectives.

Confirmation bias in web-based information processing is a complex phenomenon shaped by cognitive mechanisms, active engagement, and algorithmic personalization. Echo chambers and filter bubbles, fuelled by AI-driven personalization, limit users' exposure to diverse perspectives, reinforcing biases and contributing to social polarization. Active content creation amplifies confirmation bias, as individuals selectively recall and share information that aligns with their beliefs, strengthening the selective information cycle.

Understanding these dynamics is essential for developing strategies to mitigate the negative impacts of confirmation bias in digital environments. By exploring the cognitive and algorithmic factors that contribute to confirmation bias, this chapter underscores the need to foster critical thinking and promote cognitive diversity in digital spaces. As we navigate an increasingly connected world, addressing confirmation bias in online information processing becomes more pressing than ever before.

1.2   Impact on Decision-Making and Societal Polarization in Digital Environments

The increasing integration of artificial intelligence (AI) into social networks has profound implications for polarization, extremism, and political violence. Burton (2023) highlights how algorithms within AI systems influence the evolution and divergence of opinions within networks, exacerbating social divisions and facilitating extremism. This phenomenon, termed "algorithmic extremism," stems from flaws in AI design, the data these systems rely upon, and the ways they are deployed, all of which contribute to harmful societal outcomes. Burton emphasized that these securitization processes, which dictate how AI is conceptualized and operationalized, play a pivotal role in shaping its negative impacts. A reconceptualization of AI-enabled security is necessary, with a focus on the human, social, and psychological effects of the technology to mitigate its divisive consequences and address the underlying dynamics of polarization and radicalism. This book delves into the profound ways in which confirmation bias influences decision-making and contributes to societal polarization within digital environments. Drawing from both qualitative and quantitative perspectives, it builds on a robust theoretical foundation and conceptual framework. At the core of this foundation is the psychological phenomenon of confirmation bias, which has long been studied as a human tendency to seek information that affirms preexisting beliefs. While this cognitive bias has traditionally been observed offline, the hyperconnectivity of the digital world amplifies its effects as individuals engage with vast amounts of personalized content. Despite empirical evidence (Tversky & Kahneman, 1974) supporting the prevalence of cognitive biases in information processing, confirmation bias remains challenging to quantify universally because of the nuanced nature of digital interactions across diverse populations.

Digital platforms have a marked influence on the ways individuals process information, often reinforcing confirmation biases that shape both personal beliefs and collective attitudes. The concept of the *filter bubble*, as described by Pariser (2011), highlights how algorithms predict user preferences by tracking interactions, such as clicks and searches. Over time, these algorithms curate a selective view of the world for users, primarily showing content that aligns with their established preferences. This selective exposure creates an isolated "web of one," limiting the cognitive dissonance that might otherwise arise from encountering opposing views. In this digital landscape, platforms such as Instagram and X cultivate echo chambers, where users are repeatedly exposed to familiar perspectives, effectively deepening their biases and creating self-reinforcing cycles of belief.

Artificial intelligence (AI) systems further reinforce these biases through sophisticated algorithms that curate content on the basis of past user behaviour. AI-driven personalization presents a narrow set of perspectives, effectively reducing opportunities for users to encounter diverse viewpoints. As Schweiger and Cress (2019) reported, individuals frequently encounter information that mirrors prior behaviour, strengthening confirmation bias by continuously affirming their beliefs. Social media platforms, in particular, exacerbate this by fostering echo chambers where users primarily engage with like-minded individuals. This carefully curated exposure promotes ideological homogeneity and reinforces the cycle of selective exposure, which can contribute to widespread polarization.

Additional reinforcement can occur through source affiliation or social endorsement. Messing and Westwood (2014) demonstrated that stronger social endorsement increases the probability that people select content and that their presence reduces partisan selective exposure to levels indistinguishable from chance. The fragmentation of the media environment limits the diversity of information available to citizens (Messing & Westwood, 2014). It also polarizes individual-level attitudes (Stroud, 2010), increases ideological homogeneity among party members (or partisan sorting; see Levendusky, 2009), perpetuates the support of falsehoods (Kull et al., 2003), and alters the way consumers of partisan news sources react to threats (Baum, 2011). Messing and Westwood (2014) argued that the socialization of Internet news fundamentally alters the context in which news reading occurs, providing a venue that promotes exposure to news from politically heterogeneous individuals and that serves to emphasize social value rather than partisan affiliation. This notion proved to be wrong because it did not consider confirmation bias.

Historically, the web 2.0 design paradigm emerged (Messing & Westwood, 2014), which emphasized the importance of user-generated reviews, collaborative filtering (i.e. "people like you also like this"), and aggregated popularity ratings to effectively manage vast amounts of data (O'Reilly, 2007). The web user experience improved, and in 2005, the *New York Times* and other news media companies began to emphasize their most popular and most emailed articles on their homepages (Messing & Westwood, 2014). These aggregated social endorsements marked the beginning of an expansive effort to socialize the online news reading experience (Messing & Westwood, 2014). The sharing of news stories was simplified by clicking one button so that users of social net-working sites could see these stories as status updates from their contacts. People's confirmation bias is not challenged, as they rarely discuss issues and current events that disconfirm their attitudes (Mutz, 2004), and people are more likely to chance counter-attitudinal content in the mass media than in the context of interpersonal interactions (Mutz & Martin, 2001), such as on social networking sites.

Two significant models provide a theoretical foundation for under-standing these dynamics. The *RECRO model* by Neo (2016) outlines stages of information processing that lead to radicalization, where confirmation bias plays a key role in echo chamber formation. While this model focuses on connecting individuals with like-minded groups, it does not address the active role of users in content creation or the impact of temporal dynamics. Alternatively, the *Reflective Search Model* proposed by Seitlinger and Ley (2016) offers a cognitive framework for exploring how individuals engage with information in digital spaces. This model empha-sizes that information seeking is not a straightforward process but involves a dynamic interplay between active search actions and reflective thinking. It consists of three primary components: search action, search cognition, and search reflection.

- **The search action** involves the specific steps individuals take when searching for information, including formulating search queries and evaluating results.
- **Search cognition** focuses on the cognitive processes involved in deter-mining relevance and credibility, as users adjust strategies on the basis of encountered information.
- **Search reflection** highlights metacognitive processes, where users assess progress towards their goals and critically evaluate their search behaviours and outcomes.

Together, these components illustrate a feedback loop in which indi-viduals iteratively refine their search processes on the basis of previous actions and reflections. This model underscores the proactive role of indi-viduals within information-rich environments, where they continuously adjust their strategies and exercise critical thinking. By integrating both external actions and internal cognitive processes, the *reflective search model* provides a comprehensive understanding of information engagement in digital contexts. This research incorporates elements of this model to explore how prompts for active content creation can establish feedback loops that reinforce biases, particularly when immediate and delayed memory recall is involved. The interaction of content creation and memory retrieval has implications for bias reinforcement, especially when the timing of information exposure and content production is considered.

To address these issues, this study proposes the *TART* (Thinking-Absorption-Reinforcement-Time) model, which incorporates the influence of confirmation bias on social media platforms and aims to understand how different modes of content consumption contribute to bias reinforcement over time. The TART model comprises four phases, each with specific triggers:

1. **Thinking**—The initiation phase, where users subconsciously seek information that aligns with their beliefs. This process is influenced by the design of the digital environment and users' predispositions. The *thinking* phase aligns with the initial stage of content consumption, where selective exposure begins.
2. **Absorption**—In this passive phase, users internalize information without critical evaluation. The absence of critical thinking during content absorption often reinforces confirmation bias. This phase supports the notion that passive engagement can solidify biases, whereas active engagement may encourage more critical thought.
3. **Reinforcement**—Engagement, whether active or passive, further entrenches biases. Active engagement—such as commenting or sharing—can amplify bias by reinforcing belief consistency, whereas passive engagement maintains the status quo. This phase directly supports the study's hypothesis that active engagement intensifies confirmation bias, whereas passive engagement preserves it.
4. **Time–Temporal dynamics** influence bias reinforcement, as delayed exposure to information may allow for reflection and potential mitigation of bias, whereas immediate content creation strengthens bias. This phase emphasizes the moderating effect of temporal delay,

aligning with the study's hypothesis that the timing and frequency of exposure affect the reinforcement of confirmation bias.

These phases highlight the impact of active and passive content engagement, exploring how each contributes to confirmation bias within digital platforms. For example, *active content creation*—through posts or comments—deepens engagement with personal beliefs, reinforcing confirmation bias, whereas *passive content consumption* maintains bias at a lower, steady level. Furthermore, the TART model accounts for the impact of the frequency and timing of content exposure, illustrating how repeated encounters with similar viewpoints reinforce biases more rapidly for active content creators than for passive consumers.

This framework also considers the role of social networks in perpetuating confirmation bias. Social endorsement, such as likes and shares, increases the perceived reliability of content, leading to a reinforcement of selective exposure and contributing to ideological homogeneity. The social media-induced polarization (SMIP) model of Modgil et al. (2021) further illustrates how digital platforms drive polarization through algorithmic curation and user interactions. During significant events, such as the COVID-19 pandemic, SMIP has contributed to polarized public opinions by reinforcing confirmation bias within echo chambers. SMIP's four elements—environmental setting, actors, mechanism, and outcome—frame the interactions that intensify polarization and deepen existing biases, often limiting users' exposure to opposing viewpoints.

By introducing these theoretical foundations, this study establishes a strong framework for exploring the impact of digital environments on confirmation bias and polarization. The interaction of algorithms, user behaviour, and social endorsement creates a powerful feedback loop that not only influences individual beliefs but also affects broader societal dynamics. Through this lens, digital misinformation emerges as a significant risk, as identified by the World Economic Forum (2018), with confirmation bias serving as a driving force behind digital polarization and radicalization.

In conclusion, this book's theoretical foundation and conceptual framework provide insight into how confirmation bias operates within digital environments. Through models such as RECRO, Reflective

Search, SMIP, and TART, this research illustrates the complexity of confirmation bias reinforcement. By understanding the influence of content consumption modes, temporal factors, and algorithmic design, this study highlights strategies for reducing the effects of cognitive biases in digital interactions, ultimately fostering a more balanced and informed digital ecosystem.

1.3   Examination of Feedback Loops That Either Weaken or Strengthen Bias

In digital environments, confirmation bias often forms a feedback loop, where exposure to biased information strengthens preexisting beliefs. This reinforcing cycle is influenced by various factors, including content engagement, memory retrieval, and the timing of content creation. These feedback loops are essential for understanding how confirmation bias operates, as they can either strengthen or mitigate bias depending on how users interact with information. The findings of Trang et al. (2024) align closely with the themes of our research, particularly the role of technology in reinforcing biases and fostering feedback loops that intensify polarized thinking. Their study demonstrates how technology conspiracy beliefs not only arise from distrust in IT systems but also amplify a broader conspiracy mindset that hinders societal well-being. These insights reinforce the importance of understanding how feedback loops driven by confirmation bias, selective exposure, and algorithmic curation contribute to the proliferation of technology-related conspiracy beliefs. In the context of our research, the harmful feedback loops described by Trang et al. are exacerbated by active digital engagement, which accelerates biased information processing and deepens individuals' immersion in ideologically homogenous digital environments. This underscores the urgency of addressing these dynamics, both at the individual and systemic levels, to mitigate the broader societal consequences of digital polarization and conspiracy thinking.

AI bias is further exacerbated by user confirmation bias. When users interact with AI systems, they often prefer results that align with their existing beliefs. This confirmation bias feeds into the feedback loop of AI algorithms, which, over time, adjust to user preferences by curating content that aligns with those biases (Bozdag, 2013). Consequently, users' biases actively shape the information they are presented with, creating a cycle where both the AI's inherent biases—as mentioned earlier—and user biases reinforce each other. Addressing these sources of bias is crucial for developing AI systems that promote fair and diverse perspectives rather than intensifying existing biases.

Temporal dynamics, as highlighted by Gabielkov et al. (2016), demonstrate that the timing of exposure and engagement influences both user interaction and memory retrieval. If users encounter reinforcing information soon after initial exposure, they are more likely to retain it, thus reinforcing confirmation bias. Conversely, delayed exposure can introduce a reflective pause, which might allow individuals to question the information or engage with diverse viewpoints, thereby potentially weakening the bias.

The importance of feedback loops becomes even more apparent in the context of social endorsement. Messing and Westwood (2014) demonstrated that strong social endorsements, such as likes or shares, increase the likelihood of content selection. This validation process reinforces selective exposure by amplifying the salience and perceived reliability of the information, which in turn strengthens confirmation bias. As users encounter content validated by their social networks, these endorsements contribute to ideological homogeneity within online communities, where shared beliefs intensify over time.

The feedback loop concept, particularly within social media and online radicalization, connects directly to the processes that drive confirmation bias, reinforcement of beliefs, and polarization. Although not always explicitly addressed, models such as the RECRO model by Neo (2016) touch upon this feedback mechanism. In such scenarios, feedback loops are created as individuals repeatedly encounter similar viewpoints, reinforcing initial biases until they reach a cycle of belief reinforcement. The distinction between active and passive content creation is particularly significant in this context, as these two modes of engagement distinctly influence how confirmation bias develops.

Encouraging delayed active content creation can be a potential strategy to counteract confirmation bias, but it also presents challenges. According to Trattner et al. (2016), fostering critical thinking and promoting a reflective approach during online searches can open the door to a more balanced web environment. Moving from simple content copying to critical evaluation of diverse information can help individuals engage with their biases, leading to a more nuanced understanding. Metacognitive reflection, or the act of thinking about one's own thinking, may allow users to recognize biases in their own information-seeking behaviours, thus weakening the reinforcement loop that confirmation bias often creates. The emergence and reinforcement of conspiracy mindsets provide a stark example of how feedback loops operate in digital ecosystems. Trang et al. (2024) highlight how technology conspiracy beliefs, such as those surrounding popular commercial technologies such as Amazon Echo or public tools such as contact tracing apps, perpetuate distrust and foster broader conspiracy mindsets. These beliefs, driven by selective exposure and algorithmic curation, create a reinforcing cycle where distrust in technology leads to further isolation within ideologically similar networks. Our research extends this by examining how active digital engagement intensifies such feedback loops, with users actively seeking and promoting content that aligns with their preexisting biases. Together, these dynamics illustrate how digital environments facilitate self-reinforcing loops that deepen biases, impede the adoption of beneficial technologies, and undermine constructive social collaboration.

While active content creation offers opportunities to engage critically, it does not always guarantee a departure from bias. This is because feedback loops continue to operate on the basis of factors such as content engagement, social endorsement, and user memory retrieval. When users actively contribute thoughts or comments, they may still reinforce their beliefs by selectively interpreting information. Therefore, fostering a more diverse and reflective information ecosystem requires not only encouraging active participation but also promoting exposure to alternative viewpoints and fostering critical engagement.

Given these dynamics, feedback loops within digital environments clearly have significant implications for confirmation bias. On the one hand, they can reinforce and entrench biases, leading to stronger ideological divides. On the other hand, they can be disrupted by strategic interventions—such as encouraging metacognitive practices, providing exposure to diverse perspectives, and fostering critical evaluation—that promote awareness of cognitive biases. Ultimately, feedback loops shape how users process and retain information, influencing personal beliefs and contributing to social polarization in digital spaces.

In summary, the dynamics of confirmation bias in digital environments underscore the power of feedback loops, where biased information is either reinforced or mitigated through patterns of engagement and timing. By examining these processes, this book offers insights into how digital platforms shape cognitive biases and highlights opportunities for creating a more balanced and open information ecosystem.

References

Baltezarević, R., Baltezarević, I., & Ravić, N. (2023). Confirmation bias in digital communication: The tendency of consumers to favor information that confirms their pre-existing beliefs. *Megatrend Revija, 20*(2), 25–35. https://doi.org/10.5937/megrev2302026b

Baum, M. A. (2011). *Red, blue, and the flu: Media self-selection and partisan gaps in swine flu vaccinations.* HKS Faculty Research Working Paper Series RWP11-010. Harvard Kennedy School.

Bozdag, E. (2013). Bias in algorithmic filtering and personalization. *Ethics and Information Technology, 15*(3), 209–227.

Burton, J. (2023). Algorithmic extremism? The securitization of artificial intelligence (AI) and its impact on radicalism, polarization and political violence. *Technology in Society, 75,* 102262. https://doi.org/10.1016/j.techsoc.2023.102262

Cichocka, A., Marchlewska, M., & de Zavala, A. G. (2016). Does self-love or self-hate predict conspiracy beliefs? Narcissism, self-esteem, and the endorsement of conspiracy theories. *Social Psychological and Personality Science, 7*(2), 157–166.

Dastin, J. (2018, October 10). *Amazon scraps secret AI recruiting tool that showed bias against women.* Reuters.

Flaxman, S., Goel, S., & Rao, J. M. (2016). Filter bubbles, echo chambers, and online news consumption. *Public Opinion Quarterly, 80*(S1), 298–320. https://doi.org/10.1093/poq/nfw006

Frost, P., Casey, B., Griffin, K., Raymundo, L., Farrell, C., & Carrigan, R. (2015). The influence of confirmation bias on memory and source monitoring. *The Journal of General Psychology, 142*(4), 238–252. https://doi.org/10.1080/00221309.2015.1084987

Gabielkov, M., Ramachandran, A., Chaintreau, A., & Legout, A. (2016). Social clicks: What and who gets read on Twitter? In *Proceedings of the ACM SIGMETRICS/IFIP Performance 2016*. Antibes Juan-les-Pins, France.

Garrett, R. K. (2009). Politically motivated reinforcement seeking: Reframing the selective exposure debate. *Journal of Communication, 59*(4), 676–699.

Knobloch-Westerwick, S., Mothes, C., & Polavin, N. (2020). Confirmation bias, ingroup bias, and negativity bias in selective exposure to political information. *Communication Research, 47*(1), 104–124. https://doi.org/10.1177/0093650217719596

Kull, S., Ramsay, C., & Lewis, E. (2003). Misperceptions, the media, and the Iraq war. *Political Science Quarterly, 118*(4), 569–598. https://doi.org/10.1002/j.1538-165x.2003.tb00406.x

Lee, J. K., Choi, J., Kim, C., & Kim, Y. (2014). Social media, network heterogeneity, and opinion polarization. *Journal of Communication, 64*(4), 702–722. https://doi.org/10.1111/jcom.12077

Levendusky, M. (2009). *The partisan sort: How liberals became Democrats and conservatives became Republicans*. University of Chicago Press.

Liao, Q. V., & Fu, W. T. (2014). Can you hear me now? Mitigating the echo chamber effect by source position indicators. In *Proceedings of the 17th ACM conference on computer supported cooperative work & social computing* (pp. 184–196). Association for Computing Machinery.

Malek, M. A. (2022). Criminal courts' artificial intelligence: The way it reinforces bias and discrimination. *AI and Ethics, 2*, 233–245.

Messing, S., & Westwood, S. J. (2014). Selective exposure in the age of social media: Endorsements trump partisan source affiliation when selecting news online. *Communication Research, 41*(8), 1042–1063. https://doi.org/10.1177/0093650212466406

Modgil, S., Singh, R. K., Gupta, S., & Dennehy, D. (2021). A confirmation bias view on social media induced polarisation during Covid-19. *Information Systems Frontiers*, 1–25.

Mutz, D., & Martin, P. S. (2001). Facilitating communication across lines of political difference: The role of mass media. *American Political Science Review, 95*(1), 97–114.

Mutz, D. C. (2004). Cross-cutting social networks: Testing democratic theory in practice. *American Political Science Review, 96*(1), 111–126. https://doi.org/10.1017/s0003055402004264

Neo, L. S. (2016). An internet-mediated pathway for online radicalisation: RECRO. In *Combating violent extremism and radicalization in the digital era* (pp. 197–224).

Nickerson, R. S. (1998). Confirmation bias: A ubiquitous phenomenon in many guises. *Review of General Psychology, 2*(2), 175–220. https://doi.org/10.1037/1089-2680.2.2.175

O'Reilly, T. (2007). What is web 2.0: Design patterns and business models for the next generation of software. *Communications and Strategies, 17*, 1–17.

Pariser, E. (2011). *The filter bubble: How the new personalized web is changing what we read and how we think.* Penguin.

Pytlik, N., Soll, D., & Mehl, S. (2020). Thinking preferences and conspiracy belief: Intuitive thinking and the jumping to conclusions-bias as a basis for the belief in conspiracy theories. *Frontiers in Psychiatry, 11*, 568942. https://doi.org/10.3389/fpsyt.2020.568942

Quattrociocchi, W., Scala, A., & Sunstein, C. R. (2016). *Echo chambers on Facebook.* Harvard Law School Discussion Paper No. 877. http://www.law.harvard.edu/programs/olin_center/papers/pdf/Sunstein_877.pdf

Räikkä, J., & Basham, L. (2018). *Conspiracy theories and the people who believe them.* Oxford University Press.

Ross, L., Lepper, M. R., & Hubbard, M. (1975). Perseverance in self-perception and social perception: Biased attributional processes in the debriefing paradigm. *Journal of Personality and Social Psychology, 32*(5), 880–892. https://doi.org/10.1037/0022-3514.32.5.880

Schweiger, S., & Cress, U. (2019). How confidence in prior attitudes, social tag popularity, and source credibility shape confirmation bias toward antidepressants and psychotherapy in a representative German sample: Randomized controlled web-based study. *Journal of Medical Internet Research, 21*(4), e11081. https://doi.org/10.2196/11081

Schweiger, S., Oeberst, A., & Cress, U. (2014). Confirmation bias in web-based search: A randomized online study on the effects of expert information and social tags on information search and evaluation. *Journal of Medical Internet Research, 16*(3), e94. https://doi.org/10.2196/jmir.3044

Seitlinger, P., & Ley, T. (2016). *Reconceptualizing imitation in social tagging: A reflective search model of human web interaction.* In Proceedings of the 8th International ACM Web Science Conference 2016.

Stall, L. M., & Petrocelli, J. V. (2022). Countering conspiracy theory beliefs: Understanding the conjunction fallacy and considering disconfirming evidence. *Applied Cognitive Psychology, 37*(2), 266–276. https://doi.org/10.1002/acp.3998

Stroud, N. J. (2010). Polarization and partisan selective exposure. *Journal of Communication, 60*(3), 556–576. https://doi.org/10.1111/j.1460-2466.2010.01497.x

Sunstein, C. R. (2001). *Echo chambers: Bush v. Gore, impeachment, and beyond.* Princeton University Press.

Trang, S., Kraemer, T., Trenz, M., & Weiger, W. H. (2024). Deeper down the rabbit hole: How technology conspiracy beliefs emerge and foster a conspiracy mindset. *Information Systems Research.* https://doi.org/10.1287/isre.2022.0494

Trattner, C., Kowald, D., Seitlinger, P., Ley, T., & Kopeinik, S. (2016). Modeling activation processes in human memory to predict the use of tags in social bookmarking systems. *Journal of Web Science, 2*(1), 1–16. https://doi.org/10.1561/106.00000004

Tversky, A., & Kahneman, D. (1974). Judgment under uncertainty: Heuristics and biases. *Science, 185*(4157), 1124–1131.

Vlasceanu, M., & Amodio, D. M. (2022). Propagation of societal gender inequality by internet search algorithms. *Proceedings of the National Academy of Sciences, 119*(29), e2204529119.

Wason, P. C. (1960). On the failure to eliminate hypotheses in a conceptual task. *Quarterly Journal of Experimental Psychology, 12*(3), 129–140. https://doi.org/10.1080/17470216008416717

World Economic Forum. (2018). *Digital wildfires.* http://reports.weforum.org/global-risks-2018/digital-wildfires/

2

Algorithms, Polarization, and the Digital Age: A Literature Review

Abstract This chapter reviews the extensive literature on confirmation bias, digital echo chambers, and the role of algorithms in selectively exposing users to information. It discusses the reinforcement of cognitive biases through social media platforms, focusing on the role of artificial intelligence in curating content that aligns with users' preexisting beliefs. Key case studies, including the #BlackLivesMatter movement, illustrate the real-world impact of these phenomena. The chapter concludes by identifying gaps in the literature, such as the limited exploration of temporal dynamics and active content creation, which the study aims to address.

Keywords Algorithms • Cognitive biases • Confirmation bias • Temporal dynamics • Content creation • Digital environments • Conspiracy theory • Misinformation • Polarization • Artificial polarization

2.1   Review of Existing Literature on Confirmation Bias, Echo Chambers, and the Role of Algorithms in Curating Content

In today's interconnected digital world, individuals are especially susceptible to confirmation bias, the tendency to seek information that reinforces their preexisting beliefs. This cognitive bias can discourage engagement with diverse viewpoints, leading to deeper entrenchment of existing opinions and, in some cases, radicalization. The digital landscape intensifies these effects, providing an ideal environment for biased opinions to flourish and influence public sentiment. Notable events, such as the Cambridge Analytica scandal, highlight how confirmation bias can be manipulated for political and social gain, underscoring its relevance in domains as varied as security policy and social research. For that reason, research has increasingly focused on exploring the cognitive underpinnings of conspiracy beliefs. Studies suggest that conspiracy theory believers are more prone to cognitive biases, including jumping-to-conclusions bias and conjunction fallacy (Pytlik et al., 2020; Stall & Petrocelli, 2022). These biases, along with a preference for intuitive thinking over analytical reasoning, contribute to the formation and maintenance of conspiracy beliefs (Gagliardi, 2023; Pytlik et al., 2020). Interestingly, some researchers propose the concept of "conspiracy theory phobia," where individuals reject conspiracy theories without proper evaluation due to psychological mechanisms such as confirmation bias (Räikkä & Basham, 2018). To counter conspiracy beliefs, interventions targeting the propensity for conjunctive errors and encouraging consideration of disconfirming evidence have shown promise (Stall & Petrocelli, 2022). Understanding these cognitive processes provides valuable insights into the nature of conspiracy thinking and potential strategies for addressing it in various contexts.

Confirmation bias operates at both the individual and societal levels, impacting personal decision-making, social cohesion, and democratic discourse. This far-reaching influence necessitates a comprehensive understanding of its mechanisms and its role in digital spaces. The pressing need to address confirmation bias extends beyond personal well-being; it is crucial for maintaining the integrity of information ecosystems, guiding policy-making, and preserving the social fabric of our interconnected society.

This chapter embarks on a thorough exploration of confirmation bias and its dynamics within digital environments, particularly through the lenses of content consumption modes and temporal factors. Through rigorous examination, it aims to uncover hidden dimensions of this pervasive phenomenon and identify connections that will inform future research. By addressing gaps in current knowledge, this book strives to shed light on the intricate ways in which confirmation bias shapes cognition, behaviour, and societal outcomes.

This chapter is structured to provide an in-depth overview of confirmation bias and its role in the digital era. It covers a wide range of topics, beginning with an analysis of the cognitive mechanisms that contribute to the reinforcement of preexisting beliefs. Additionally, it examines how digital platforms intensify the effects of confirmation bias, referencing historical examples to underscore the potential for manipulation and the need for vigilance. The chapter also explores the societal implications of confirmation bias, from its influence on public opinion to its significance in shaping security policies and research agendas. It concludes by identifying areas within the study of confirmation bias that warrant further investigation, thereby establishing a foundation for the book's unique contributions.

People "hear their own voice" in echo chambers (Boutyline & Willer, 2017; Flaxman et al., 2016). This means that only the content of like-minded users and/or views is consumed in the context of social media (Bessi, 2016; Geschke et al., 2019). Most recent studies have focused on the effects of confirmation bias and echo chambers such as polarization (Modgil et al., 2021). According to Whittaker (2020), digital platforms significantly contribute to the stages of confirmation, reinforcement, and polarization in the process of radicalization. Whittaker (2020) claims that there is no clear, conceptual definition in regard to the term "echo chamber" and that many scholars are using it incorrectly or without putting it into context. Whittaker (2020) describes the two meanings that can be inferred from the use of the term "echo chambers," with the first being directly linked to confirmation bias and the second being the personalization of Internet technologies, called the "Filter Bubble" (Pariser, 2011), which is artificial polarization. These two phenomena have similar outcomes; however, they differ in their causes (Whittaker, 2020), with the former being user-driven and the latter being platform-driven. These concepts can influence each other, making it difficult to determine which of the effects are responsible for the echo chamber effect (Whittaker, 2020). According to Gabielkov et al. (2016), more than half of the articles shared on Twitter (X) are shared without the user reading them, let alone thinking critically about them, which suggests that people rely on their confirmation-biased processing of such information circulating within their trusted network.

In a study conducted by Suzuki and Yamamoto (2021) titled "Characterizing the Influence of Confirmation Bias on Web Search Behavior," the researchers aimed to investigate how confirmation bias affects web search behaviour, particularly in relation to health-related search topics. To explore this, they manipulated participants' prior beliefs about health search topics and analysed their behavioural logs during web search tasks. The researchers controlled for confirmation bias by altering participants' impressions of health search topics via prior information. The study's findings revealed several circumstances related to confirmation bias and web search behaviour. Users with poor health literacy and negative prior beliefs tended to avoid examining the list of web search results. Instead, they displayed bias in their webpage selection. Conversely, users with high health literacy and negative prior beliefs spent more time examining the list of search results. They were also more inclined to explore webpages that presented diverse opinions. Web searchers with confirmation bias preferentially browse information that is consistent with their beliefs and do not thoroughly examine the information. Web searchers with confirmation bias view only information aligned with their beliefs and do not engage in careful browsing, resulting in fewer webpages being viewed. Unlike users without confirmation bias, web searchers with confirmation bias tend not to significantly change their beliefs through web searches. The degree of confirmation bias effects is influenced by the web search user's level of information literacy. We used some adapted elements for our study. Here, the study focused on browsing and searching behaviour, involving a multistep procedure. The participants registered and completed a prior belief questionnaire. They were then exposed to prior information about the search topic, followed by the actual search task. After the task, the participants answered a post-task questionnaire. The researchers tracked variables such as dwell time on search engine results pages, dwell time on webpages, search session time, and clickthrough rates of search results. They also measured belief change before and after web searches. While the study provided valuable insights into the influence of confirmation bias on web search behaviour, there were certain aspects that the research did not address. These include factors such as time for reflection, creating content, building predictors for determining health literacy, and potential strategies for mitigating confirmation bias during web searches (e.g. using chat bots to present opposing results). While we could not include all of these factors in our studies, we incorporated some of them, such as actively creating content. The role of confirmation bias in decision-making has been widely explored, with evidence suggesting that it often leads to selective information processing that aligns with preexisting beliefs (Bergerot et al., 2024). While traditionally considered a cognitive limitation, recent studies have highlighted conditions under which moderate confirmation bias can benefit collective decision-making. For example, Bergerot et al. (2024) reported that in agent-based simulations via a collective asymmetric reinforcement learning model, moderate confirmation bias enhances group learning and decision-making in resource-scarce environments. However, excessive confirmation bias led to polarization and suboptimal performance, particularly in smaller groups. These findings suggest that the effects of confirmation bias are context dependent and influenced by factors such as group size, resource availability, and the dynamics of information exchange. In digital environments, where active engagement often intensifies confirmation bias, the implications for collective decision-making remain less clear, particularly when individual behaviours diverge from the dynamics observed in controlled simulations.

The study by Vedejová and Čavojová (2022) stands out as a comprehensive examination of confirmation bias across various stages of reasoning, including information search, interpretation, and memory recall. To address a gap in existing research, where these components are rarely studied together, Vedejová and Čavojová (2022) sought to explore the interplay of these facets within a unified paradigm. Their study focused on the impact of confirmation bias on hypothesis testing, particularly how individuals' preexisting beliefs shape their engagement with information related to controversial topics such as stem cell research, the death penalty, gun legalization, and compulsory school uniforms.

By employing a methodology in which participants were tasked with assisting a friend's decision-making in reference to these topics, the researchers utilized a real-world approach. The participants used Google to search for information, engaging with titles and descriptions from various perspectives (pro, con, neutral) to simulate a realistic information search process. This approach allowed the study to capture the nuances of confirmation bias in a naturalistic setting, shedding light on how motivational components influence information processing.

The findings from Vedejová and Čavojová's (2022) study contribute significantly to the understanding of confirmation bias, emphasizing its multifaceted nature and the importance of considering motivational aspects in its measurement. Despite its innovative approach, the study has limitations, such as the use of a recognition task for memory recall, which may not fully capture the spontaneous recall of information that aligns with participants' preexisting beliefs. This suggests avenues for future research to explore more nuanced methods of measuring memory recall. In summary, Vedejová and Čavojová's (2022) research provides critical insight into the dynamics of confirmation bias in information processing and decision-making, which influenced the setup of our study, where we added the active content creation factor to fully incorporate this missing task.

The phenomenon of confirmation bias in digital interactions, particularly in the context of social tagging, provides a valuable framework for understanding how cognitive processes manifest online. Seitlinger and Ley's (2016) *Reflective Search Model* challenges traditional views of tagging behaviour as merely social imitation. Instead, tagging is a reflective process shaped by episodic and semantic memory, suggesting that tag choices are influenced by both cognitive structures and web interactions. This model reveals that the stabilization of social tags within a community often occurs as a side effect of individual reflection rather than imitation, shifting the focus to a cognitive understanding of tagging and social categorization.

Integrating Seitlinger and Ley's reflective search model into the context of confirmation bias allows us to see how biases in information retrieval and categorization are not just social but are deeply rooted in individual cognitive and memory processes. This perspective expands our understanding of confirmation bias in digital environments, offering insights into web interface design that could support more accurate and diverse information retrieval, ultimately mitigating bias.

The reflective search model serves as a fitting theoretical foundation for this book, aligning well with its research questions and objectives. By examining the reflective and temporal aspects of content creation, the model provides a unique lens through which to explore the ways in which active engagement and timing may impact confirmation bias, highlighting potential debiasing effects.

Confirmation bias has also been studied extensively in the context of social media, where its influence is particularly evident in hashtag usage on platforms such as X. Lex et al. (2018) examined hashtag reuse within personal networks, revealing that users overwhelmingly prefer the hashtags they encounter within their social circles. This practice strengthens filter bubbles, creating environments where users are primarily exposed to familiar views. Their study revealed that 66% to 81% of hashtag assignments stemmed from individual or social hashtag reuse, illustrating how confirmation bias shapes discourse on X and limits exposure to alternative perspectives.

Lex et al. (2018) also identified the temporal aspect of hashtag reuse and noted that users are more likely to reuse recently encountered hashtags, especially within a 24-hour period. This observation suggests that confirmation bias and filter bubbles are influenced not only by content but also by the timing of encounters, reinforcing the cycle of biased information consumption. To mitigate this, the authors propose algorithms that balance accuracy with diversity, introducing contrasting viewpoints to break filter bubbles and encourage broader information exposure. Their work has implications for social media design, where an understanding of confirmation bias could inspire more inclusive and diverse spaces that support a range of perspectives.

In the current digital landscape, social media-induced polarization (SMIP) has become a key area of focus, particularly during global crises such as the COVID-19 pandemic. Modgil et al. (2021) provide an in-depth analysis of SMIP, showing how social media fosters polarization through mechanisms of confirmation bias and echo chambers. Their study revealed that social media algorithms create reinforcing feedback loops, which amplify users' existing beliefs and contribute to increasingly homogenized and ideologically distinct communities. This model is integral to this book's theoretical framework, as it highlights how feedback loops and polarizing effects operate before and after users are exposed to confirmatory content.

By incorporating Modgil et al.'s (2021) findings on SMIP, this book emphasizes the crucial role of social media in shaping perceptions and decision-making. The concept of SMIP provides a nuanced understanding of the risks associated with digital polarization and underscores the need for responsible digital platform design that mitigates radicalization and promotes constructive discourse.

Together, these theoretical insights provide a comprehensive framework for exploring confirmation bias in digital environments. By examining models such as the Reflective Search Model, Kowald and Lex's study on hashtag dynamics, and SMIP, this book establishes a solid foundation for understanding the complex interplay between cognitive processes, social algorithms, and information polarization. This approach illuminates the potential for designing platforms that support critical thinking and broaden users' perspectives, fostering a digital landscape that balances user engagement with exposure to diverse ideas.

2.2   Analysis of Social Media's Role in Radicalization, with Case Studies Such as #BlackLivesMatter

In the evolving landscape of terrorism and radicalization, digital platforms have become central to self-radicalization. Wylde's (2020) work *The Digital Age Cyber Space and Social Media: The Challenges of Security & Radicalization* underscores this shift, particularly focusing on self-radicalization through social media. Influenced by Neo's (2016) contributions and other researchers, Wylde highlights a trend where individuals are exposed to extremist ideologies online, fostering a type of radicalization that poses new challenges for law enforcement and national security.

Historically, terrorism was viewed as a primarily domestic issue within the United States; however, after 9/11, the focus expanded to include Islamic extremism with a global reach. This shift reflects the changing nature of radicalization, particularly as the Internet and social media allow for the rapid spread of extremist ideologies. The Internet's role has become vital in facilitating radicalization, allowing individuals to connect and engage with extremist groups without the need for physical contact or traditional recruitment. This phenomenon represents a marked departure from past forms of radicalization, where individuals travel to training camps or meet directly with extremist groups.

Wylde (2020) also examines how platforms such as Facebook, Twitter, and YouTube serve as tools for disseminating propaganda and recruiting followers. Groups such as ISIS use these platforms to spread their messages, reaching potential recruits across the globe. Self-radicalization via digital channels allows for anonymity, enabling individuals to explore and eventually embrace extremist ideologies with little outside interference.

Neo's (2016) RECRO model, as detailed in Wylde's work, offers a framework for understanding the stages of radicalization, particularly in the context of antivaccination conspiracies. This model describes a five-phase progression from initial doubts to active endorsement and dissemination of conspiratorial content:

1. Reflection phase: Here, individuals begin to question or hesitate on issues—such as vaccine safety—on the basis of factors such as distrust or concerns over personal freedom. These doubts make them more susceptible to anti-vaccine narratives.
2. Exploration phase: In this stage, individuals actively seek information that aligns with their initial doubts. Confirmation bias plays a central role, as people gravitate towards weak evidence that reinforces their scepticism.
3. Connection phase: Individuals form or join communities, often facilitated by social media, that validate and amplify their beliefs. This phase strengthens the echo chamber effect, isolating it from alternative perspectives.
4. Reinforcement phase: At this stage, the individual's scepticism solidifies into a firm belief system through continuous interaction with conspiratorial content. Social media echo chambers reinforce these beliefs, particularly as users encounter stories, often misleading, that seem to confirm their views.
5. Outreach phase: In the final stage, individuals actively disseminate anti-vaccine or extremist ideologies, aiming to influence others. This phase includes sharing narratives, promoting controversial studies, and advocating for alternative practices over vaccination.

The RECRO model provides a valuable framework for understanding the mechanisms by which digital platforms contribute to radicalization. It illustrates how echo chambers on social media amplify and solidify extremist beliefs, offering insights into how confirmation bias operates in these contexts.

Research indicates that social media users tend to form polarized groups around shared beliefs, reinforcing their existing views through selective exposure to information (Quattrociocchi et al., 2016). This phenomenon, known as the echo chamber effect, is driven by confirmation bias, where users prefer and share content that aligns with their preexisting opinions (Garrett, 2009). Studies have shown that users not only seek reinforcing information but also avoid challenging viewpoints, leading to the formation of distinct, polarized communities (Brugnoli et al., 2019). The emergence of AI-powered search systems, particularly those utilizing large language models (LLMs), may exacerbate this issue by increasing biased information querying and selective exposure (Sharma et al., 2024). These findings highlight the potential risks associated with AI-driven information systems in reinforcing echo chambers and limiting exposure to diverse perspectives, raising concerns about their impact on public discourse and opinion formation in the digital age.

Confirmation bias in online information consumption has been a focal point for researchers aiming to understand how digital environments shape belief systems. Festinger's (1957) theory of cognitive dissonance explains individuals' preference for information that aligns with their existing beliefs—a phenomenon that is only magnified in today's digital ecosystem. According to Duffy et al. (2020), as people increasingly turn to social media for news, they encounter confirmation bias more frequently, reinforcing their beliefs without the balanced perspectives offered by traditional news outlets.

The online environment, particularly social networks, serves as fertile ground for confirmation bias and selective exposure. Knobloch-Westerwick's (2015) review of related studies shows that users consistently favour information that aligns with their beliefs, a trend that extends to politically charged movements such as Black Lives Matter (BLM), where users engage with content in ways that echo their own perspectives.

Furthermore, Snelson's (1993) concept of the "ideological immune system" frames confirmation bias as a psychological shield that protects individuals from conflicting beliefs, whereas Morton's (2002) "Morton's Demon" illustrates how people selectively accept supporting evidence and dismiss contradictory information. In the digital age, this concept has new relevance to the social media-induced polarization (SMIP) framework proposed by Modgil et al. (2021), which highlights how confirmation bias and echo chambers on social media reinforce individuals' existing beliefs, contributing to the formation of polarized communities.

Within this digital landscape, confirmation bias becomes increasingly problematic. Social media platforms enable users to share, post, and tag information that aligns with their views, which reinforces selective exposure and intensifies biases. As Tim Cook and other industry leaders have cautioned, misinformation spreads rapidly on social media, amplifying confirmation bias as users actively participate in creating and endorsing biased content. Studies by Phan et al. (2019) and Shin and Thorson (2017) emphasize how the filtered nature of information on social media keeps users within bubbles that validate their perspectives.

The active participation of social media users—whether through content creation or sharing—further intensifies confirmation bias. This engagement fosters a self-reinforcing cycle of selective exposure, leading to radicalization in some cases. In endorsing content sharing, social media perpetuates the effects of confirmation bias, as users circulate information that reflects their beliefs and those of their immediate network.

The study of confirmation bias within online engagement and social movements is a multidisciplinary field that incorporates insights from psychology, communication, and digital media studies. Patnaude et al. (2021) highlight the role of social media and mobile technology in sentiment analysis, particularly within the context of social movements. Their research demonstrated how language and sentiment classification can effectively identify and categorize user tweets, revealing both positive and negative sentiments. This type of analysis offers a window into the diverse perspectives and experiences related to social movements, with the Black Lives Matter (BLM) movement providing a compelling example.

The BLM movement, propelled by the #BlackLivesMatter hashtag, underscores the power of social media virality in shaping public discourse and fostering engagement. According to Patnaude et al. (2021), hashtags such as #BlackLivesMatter serve as a gateway to multiple perspectives, giving users access to a broad range of voices and viewpoints. The widespread use of this hashtag enabled individuals to explore and engage with a variety of posts, each reflecting different narratives and emotional responses. With intense news coverage and heightened emotional investment from the public, the BLM movement has drawn significant attention in both digital and traditional media spaces (Patnaude et al., 2021; Pew Research Center, 2020).

Despite the extensive literature on sentiment analysis, online engagement, and social movements, there is a notable gap in examining how confirmation bias functions within this context. Few studies delve into the complex relationship between selective exposure—driven by confirmation bias—and factors such as temporal dynamics. Although radicalization models have been adapted for related studies, there is limited exploration of how confirmation bias is reinforced specifically through social network dynamics in movements such as BLM.

The BLM movement, therefore, serves as an invaluable case for this study because of its virality, emotional resonance (both positive and negative), and pervasive news presence. This case study offers an opportunity to investigate how users' interactions with hashtag-driven content intersect with confirmation bias, allowing for new insights into selective exposure and sentiment formation. By focusing on this movement, our study contributes to the broader discourse on confirmation bias, digital engagement, and the nuanced dynamics of information consumption in the context of social movements.

In conclusion, the literature highlights confirmation bias as a pervasive issue in the digital age that is significantly magnified by social media's influence on information consumption and engagement. The dual role of confirmation bias in both passive consumption and active participation raises important questions about its impact on beliefs, behaviours, and societal discourse, particularly within the context of social movements such as Black Lives Matter (BLM). The virality of the #BlackLivesMatter hashtag exemplifies how social media platforms can reinforce selective exposure, allowing individuals to engage with content that aligns with their preexisting views. This interaction not only deepens personal biases but also shapes collective narratives and emotional responses within public discourse.

As the digital landscape evolves, understanding confirmation bias remains critical to analysing its impact on both individual cognition and broader societal trends. Our study builds on these insights by replicating passive and active consumption modes, which prompt groups to either passively consume or actively engage with content, including BLM-related materials. This approach enables us to examine how different modes of engagement influence confirmation bias, providing a foundation for a deeper understanding of how social media dynamics shape opinions and reinforce societal polarization.

2.3   Exploration of the Influence of Artificial Intelligence on Reinforcing Selective Exposure to Biased Information

Artificial intelligence plays a critical role in reinforcing selective exposure to biased information through algorithmically driven "filter bubbles," as demonstrated in the context of YouTube's influence in South Korea (Park & Park, 2024). YouTube's recommendation algorithms curate a personalized information environment for users, predominantly suggesting content aligned with their viewing habits and interactions. This process exacerbates confirmation bias, as individuals are repeatedly exposed to ideologically similar content that reinforces their preexisting beliefs. Such selective exposure leads to the "echo chamber effect," where diverse perspectives are systematically excluded, contributing to polarization and narrowing the range of viewpoints users encounter. Moreover, Park and Park's study highlights the role of network dynamics, such as the relationships between videos, channels, and commenters, in shaping collective polarization. The patterns of interaction within these conversation networks further intensify the alignment of beliefs, as commenters engage in discussions that often validate and amplify shared viewpoints. This interplay of algorithmic filtering and social dynamics underscores how artificial intelligence facilitates polarization by reinforcing cognitive biases and limiting perspective diversity within online ecosystems. Recent research highlights the potential of artificial intelligence, particularly large language models (LLMs), to reinforce selective exposure to biased information. Sharma et al. (2024) reported that LLM-powered conversational search systems led to more biased information querying than did conventional search systems, with opinionated LLMs exacerbating this bias. This aligns with earlier findings by Garrett (2009), who demonstrated that people prefer opinion-reinforcing political information online without necessarily avoiding opposing views. Westerwick et al. (2017) further explored this confirmation bias, showing that it persists regardless of source quality and can lead to attitude polarization over time. These studies suggest that AI-driven information systems may amplify existing tendencies towards selective exposure, potentially creating "generative echo chambers" (Sharma et al., 2024). As LLM-powered search becomes more prevalent, these findings have critical implications for technology development and policy-making to mitigate the risks of increased opinion polarization and limited exposure to diverse viewpoints. Artificial intelligence, particularly explainable AI (XAI), has become an influential factor in how users process information and develop biases. By providing explanations for AI-driven decisions, such as predictions in financial or real estate contexts, XAI aims to increase transparency. However, research by Bauer et al. (2023) highlights a nuanced challenge: while explanations help users understand decision factors, they also encourage confirmation bias, particularly when these explanations align with users' preconceptions. In controlled studies, users who received feature-based explanations were more likely to adjust their beliefs and decision-making patterns in line with the logic of AI. This adjustment often leads users to reinforce prior biases, favouring information that aligns with their existing mental models, which can result in biased or suboptimal decisions. For example, explanations in AI systems applied to real estate pricing led industry experts to overemphasize certain attributes, such as competitiveness, when their expectations were confirmed, even at the expense of accuracy. This interaction between XAI and user biases suggests that while explanations can clarify AI processes, they also risk reinforcing biases, especially among confident users, potentially influencing behaviour across related contexts. Addressing this dual effect is essential for harnessing AI's potential without exacerbating social and cognitive biases.

Artificial intelligence systems, particularly those using explainable AI (XAI) techniques, are designed to clarify decision-making processes by providing users with explanations about which features contribute to a given prediction. This transparency aims to make AI outputs more understandable and trustworthy. However, as Bauer et al. (2023) illustrate, XAI does not eliminate bias; instead, it can subtly reshape user perceptions and reinforce confirmation bias in ways that impact both situational information processing and longer-term mental models. When explanations are presented, users are likely to adjust their understanding of relevant features on the basis of how these explanations align with or contradict their prior beliefs. This alignment is critical: when explanations confirm users' existing mental models, individuals are more inclined to integrate the AI logic into their own, amplifying preexisting biases. Conversely, when explanations challenge entrenched beliefs, users often resist adjusting their mental models, preferring to maintain their original views even if they are less accurate. The study revealed that real estate professionals using XAI for price estimations placed undue weight on familiar attributes such as competitiveness if the AI explanations aligned with this preconception, even when this led to suboptimal decisions. This effect highlights a broader cognitive tendency where users interact with XAI: they selectively incorporate information that reinforces their biases while overlooking contradictory evidence, leading to skewed decision-making patterns over time.

This phenomenon has significant implications for web-based information processing, as it demonstrates that XAI, while intended to promote fairness and transparency, may inadvertently contribute to the entrenchment of biased beliefs. In cases where AI explanations align with users' existing biases, such as favouring certain demographic traits in hiring or prioritizing specific investment criteria, the reinforcing feedback loop of confirmation bias becomes even more entrenched, not only affecting the immediate decision but also influencing behaviours and judgements in related areas. The study suggests that XAI can lead users to over-refer to the AI's perspective, internalizing its patterns as a form of "learned bias," which may ripple outwards, reinforcing cognitive and social biases across domains. For this reason, developing AI systems that not only explain but also challenge users' assumptions will be essential in mitigating confirmation bias and promoting critical engagement with digital information sources.

Similarly, abductive reasoning, a key component in design thinking, supports innovative problem finding by allowing for the generation of hypotheses in ambiguous and complex problem spaces (Garbuio & Lin, 2021). Unlike traditional deductive or inductive approaches, abduction explores potential explanations for surprising observations, making it valuable in uncovering previously unrecognized problems and sparking creative solutions. However, cognitive barriers, including confirmation bias, can limit the effectiveness of abductive reasoning by reinforcing familiar patterns and restricting creative exploration. On a positive note, by processing large volumes of information and offering diverse perspectives, AI could increase both the speed and quality of idea generation in uncertain problem spaces, effectively supporting more unbiased and expansive problem-finding approaches in areas such as design thinking (Garbuio & Lin, 2021).

The phenomenon of individuals "hearing their own voice" in digital echo chambers (Boutyline & Willer, 2017; Flaxman et al., 2016) illustrates how social media fosters environments where people primarily consume content aligned with like-minded users and perspectives (Bessi, 2016; Geschke et al., 2019). Studies have shown that this form of selective exposure exacerbates polarization, with recent research (Modgil et al., 2021) illustrating the role of echo chambers in strengthening confirmation bias. According to Whittaker (2020), digital platforms actively contribute to the stages of confirmation, reinforcement, and polarization within the radicalization process. Whittaker further critiques the lack of a precise, conceptual definition of "echo chambers," noting that many scholars either misuse the term or fail to contextualize it. Whittaker clarifies that the term can have two distinct meanings: one directly linked to confirmation bias and another describing the "filter bubble" effect (Pariser, 2011), an artificial polarization driven by personalization algorithms. While both methods result in similar outcomes, their causes differ—echo chambers are user driven, whereas filter bubbles are platform driven. These two forces can also intersect, making it challenging to isolate the effects of each on the echo chamber phenomenon. For example, Gabielkov et al. (2016) reported that more than half of the articles shared on Twitter were shared without users reading them, let alone critically analysing them, suggesting that individuals often rely on confirmation-biased interpretations of information shared within their trusted networks.

In "Characterizing the influence of confirmation bias on web search behavior," Suzuki and Yamamoto (2021) explore how confirmation bias influences online search behaviour, particularly for health-related topics. By manipulating participants' prior beliefs and analysing their search behaviour, they found that users with low health literacy and negative preconceptions tended to avoid scrutinizing diverse sources in search results. Instead, they displayed a preference for sources aligning with their biases. Conversely, those with higher health literacy and opposing beliefs showed greater openness to examining diverse perspectives. The study highlighted the influence of confirmation bias in web searches, noting that search behaviour is significantly shaped by users' prior beliefs and information literacy. Although the study provided valuable insights, it did not explore the role of active content creation, reflection time, or predictors of health literacy, which remain areas for further research. Our study integrates some of these elements, particularly the active creation of content, to expand on these findings.

Vedejová and Čavojová's (2022) study offers a comprehensive examination of confirmation bias across various reasoning stages, including information search, interpretation, and memory recall. Using a real-world approach, participants were asked to support a friend's decision-making in referendums about contentious topics. By engaging with various perspectives (pro, con, and neutral), the study aimed to simulate realistic search behaviour and analyse confirmation bias in naturalistic settings. Their findings underscore the multifaceted nature of confirmation bias, especially the motivational components that shape information processing. However, the study acknowledges that its reliance on recognition tasks for memory recall may not fully capture spontaneous recall tendencies aligned with preexisting beliefs. This study influenced our inclusion of active content creation as an essential task, recognizing its potential to provide a more complete picture of confirmation bias.

The interplay between echo chambers, confirmation bias, and temporal dynamics within online environments has profound implications for understanding how biases are reinforced. Sageman (2004) initially explored echo chambers in the context of terrorism, identifying how closed networks of like-minded individuals can foster radicalization. Expanding on this concept, our research investigates how active content creation, coupled with temporal factors, intensifies confirmation bias. Although prior studies have examined the duration of time spent online (Wojcieszak, 2008), few have addressed the effects of delayed exposure on bias reinforcement.

Whittaker (2020) discussed how echo chambers reinforce existing beliefs, contributing to polarization, whereas Krasodomski-Jones (2017) reported that political supporters on Twitter interact primarily with ideologically similar users. These findings suggest that temporal dynamics play crucial roles in the formation and maintenance of echo chambers. By integrating three feedback loops, this study aims to provide new insights into how temporal delays shape confirmation bias, addressing an underexplored area in the current literature.

A social network perspective is essential for understanding confirmation bias, as individuals' interactions with their networks influence information processing and belief formation. Ling (2020) noted that while most research emphasizes cognitive and motivational factors in confirmation bias, social network dynamics are comparatively underexplored. On platforms such as Twitter (now "X"), hashtag-driven conversations create digital echo chambers, where confirmation bias is continually reinforced.

The cognitive basis of confirmation bias is well documented, with dual-process models by Kahneman (2011) and Stanovich (1999) categorizing cognitive processing into automatic (System 1) and deliberate (System 2) modes. System 1 thinking often predisposes individuals to confirmation bias, as they unconsciously adopt information that aligns with preexisting beliefs. By merging cognitive theories with social network perspectives, this study seeks to illuminate how confirmation bias is shaped within digital contexts. This approach provides a nuanced framework for examining confirmation bias, bridging cognitive processes with the social network effects that reinforce them.

The literature provides a broad foundation for examining confirmation bias development and reinforcement, from a general cognitive perspective to its role in social network-driven radicalization. Models such as SMIP and RECRO outline how individuals' digital behaviours shape information consumption, yet a comprehensive integration of confirmation bias, temporal dynamics, and active content creation within a single framework is rare. Furthermore, the impact of delayed exposure remains an area with limited research, underscoring a gap in understanding how temporal factors affect bias reinforcement.

This study addresses these gaps by exploring confirmation bias within the Black Lives Matter (BLM) movement on Twitter (now "X"). By examining how users' biases evolve over time and as they actively engage with content, our research provides fresh insights into confirmation bias dynamics in online spaces. Through the synthesis of multiple theories and digital behaviour frameworks, this study extends the existing knowledge by offering a comprehensive model that incorporates confirmation bias, temporal dynamics, and engagement modes. The following chapter outlines the research methodology used to examine these dynamics, detailing the design, data collection, and analysis techniques that guided this investigation.

References

Bauer, K., Von Zahn, M., & Hinz, O. (2023). Expl(AI)ned: The impact of explainable artificial intelligence on users' information processing. *Information Systems Research, 34*(4), 1582–1602. https://doi.org/10.1287/isre.2023.1199

Bergerot, C., Barfuss, W., & Romanczuk, P. (2024). *Moderate confirmation bias enhances collective decision-making in reinforcement-learning agents.* bioRxiv 2023.2011. 2021.568073.

Bessi, A. (2016). Personality traits and echo chambers on Facebook. *Computers in Human Behavior, 65*, 319–324. https://doi.org/10.1016/j.chb.2016.08.016

Boutyline, A., & Willer, R. (2017). The social structure of political echo chambers: Variation in ideological homophily in online networks. *Political Psychology, 38*(3), 551–569. https://doi.org/10.1111/pops.12337

Brugnoli, E., Cinelli, M., Quattrociocchi, W., & Scala, A. (2019). Recursive patterns in online echo chambers. *Scientific Reports, 9*, 20118.

Duffy, A., Tandoc, E., & Ling, R. (2020). Too good to be true, too good not to share: The social utility of fake news. *Information, Communication & Society, 23*(13), 1965–1979.

Festinger, L. (1957). *A theory of cognitive dissonance.* Stanford University Press.

Flaxman, S., Goel, S., & Rao, J. M. (2016). Filter bubbles, echo chambers, and online news consumption. *Public Opinion Quarterly, 80*(S1), 298–320. https://doi.org/10.1093/poq/nfw006

Gabielkov, M., Ramachandran, A., Chaintreau, A., & Legout, A. (2016). Social clicks: What and who gets read on Twitter? In *Proceedings of the 2016 ACM SIGMETRICS international conference on measurement and modeling of computer science* (pp. 179–192). Association for Computing Machinery.

Gagliardi, L. (2023). The role of cognitive biases in conspiracy beliefs: A literature review. *Journal of Economic Surveys, 39*(1), 32–65.

Garbuio, M., & Lin, N. (2021). Innovative idea generation in problem finding: Abductive reasoning, cognitive impediments, and the promise of artificial intelligence. *Journal of Product Innovation Management, 38*(6), 701–725. https://doi.org/10.1111/jpim.12602

Garrett, R. K. (2009). Politically motivated reinforcement seeking: Reframing the selective exposure debate. *Journal of Communication, 59*(4), 676–699.

Geschke, D., Lorenz, J., & Holtz, P. (2019). The triple-filter bubble: Using agent-based modelling to test a meta-theoretical framework for the emergence of filter bubbles and echo chambers. *The British Journal of Social Psychology, 58*(1), 129–149. https://doi.org/10.1111/bjso.12286

Kahneman, D. (2011). *Thinking, fast and slow.* Macmillan.

Knobloch-Westerwick, S. (2015). The selective exposure self- and affect-management (SESAM) model: Applications in the realms of race, politics, and health. *Communication Research, 42*(7), 959–985.

Krasodomski-Jones, A. (2017). *Talking to ourselves? Political debate online and the echo chamber effect.* Demos.

Lex, E., Wagner, M., & Kowald, D. (2018). *Mitigating confirmation bias on Twitter by recommending opposing views.* arXiv:1809.03901.

Ling, R. (2020). Confirmation bias in the era of mobile news consumption: The social and psychological dimensions. *Digital Journalism, 8*(5), 596–604.

Modgil, S., Singh, R. K., Gupta, S., & Dennehy, D. (2021). A confirmation bias view on social media induced polarisation during Covid-19. *Information Systems Frontiers*, 1–25.

Morton, G. R. (2002). *Morton's demon.* Retrieved from http://home.entouch.net/dmd/mortonsdemon.htm

Neo, L. S. (2016). *An Internet-Mediated Pathway for Online Radicalisation: RECRO.* https://doi.org/10.4018/978-1-5225-0156-5.ch011

Pariser, E. (2011). *The filter bubble: How the new personalized web is changing what we read and how we think.* Penguin.

Park, H. W., & Park, S. (2024). The filter bubble generated by artificial intelligence algorithms and the network dynamics of collective polarization on YouTube: The case of South Korea. *Asian Journal of Communication, 34*(2), 195–212. https://doi.org/10.1080/01292986.2024.2315584

Patnaude, L., Lomakina, C. V., Patel, A., & Bizel, G. (2021). Public emotional response on the black lives matter movement in the summer of 2020 as analyzed through Twitter. *International Journal of Marketing Studies, 13*(1), 69. https://doi.org/10.5539/ijms.v13n1p69

Pew Research Center. (2020, June 10). *Use of the #BlackLivesMatter hashtag hits record levels amid global protests over George Floyd's death while in police custody.* Pew Research Center. https://www.pewresearch.org/fact-tank/2020/06/10/

blacklivesmatter-surges-on-twitter-after-george-floyds-death/ ft_2020-06-10_blm_01_new/

Phan, N.-Q., Lee, S.-H., Jang, J. W., & Gim, G. Y. (2019). A study of group-think in online community. In R. Lee (Ed.), *Computational science/Intelligence & applied informatics* (pp. 149–168). Springer International Publishing.

Pytlik, N., Soll, D., & Mehl, S. (2020). Thinking preferences and conspiracy belief: Intuitive thinking and the jumping to conclusions-bias as a basis for the belief in conspiracy theories. *Frontiers in Psychiatry, 11*, 568942. https://doi.org/10.3389/fpsyt.2020.568942

Quattrociocchi, W., Scala, A., & Sunstein, C. R. (2016). *Echo chambers on Facebook*. Harvard Law School Discussion Paper No. 877. http://www.law.harvard.edu/programs/olin_center/papers/pdf/Sunstein_877.pdf

Räikkä, J., & Basham, L. (2018). *Conspiracy theories and the people who believe them*. Oxford University Press.

Sageman, M. (2004). *Understanding terror networks*. University of Pennsylvania Press.

Seitlinger, P., & Ley, T. (2016). Reconceptualizing imitation in social tagging: A reflective search model of human web interaction. In *Proceedings of the 8th ACM conference on web science* (pp. 146–155). Association for Computing Machinery.

Sharma, N., Liao, Q. V., & Xiao, Z. (2024). Generative echo chamber? Effect of LLM-powered search systems on diverse information seeking. In *Proceedings of the 2024 CHI Conference on Human Factors in Computing Systems*. Association for Computing Machinery.

Shin, J., & Thorson, K. (2017). Partisan selective sharing: The biased diffusion of fact-checking messages on social media. *Journal of Communication, 67*(2), 233–255. https://doi.org/10.1111/jcom.12284

Snelson, J. S. (1993). The ideological immune system: Resistance to new ideas in science. *Skeptic, 1*(4), 444–455.

Stall, L. M., & Petrocelli, J. V. (2022). Countering conspiracy theory beliefs: Understanding the conjunction fallacy and considering disconfirming evidence. *Applied Cognitive Psychology, 37*(2), 266–276. https://doi.org/10.1002/acp.3998

Stanovich, K. E. (1999). *Who is rational? Studies of individual differences in reasoning*. Psychology Press.

Suzuki, M., & Yamamoto, Y. (2021). Characterizing the influence of confirmation bias on web search behavior. *Frontiers in Psychology, 12*, 771948. https://doi.org/10.3389/fpsyg.2021.771948

Vedejová, D., & Čavojová, V. (2022). Confirmation bias in information search, interpretation, and memory recall: Evidence from reasoning about four controversial topics. *Thinking & Reasoning, 28*(1), 1–28. https://doi.org/1 0.1080/13546783.2021.1891967

Westerwick, A., Johnson, B. K., & Knobloch-Westerwick, S. (2017). Confirmation biases in selective exposure to political online information: Source bias versus content bias. *Communication Monographs, 84*(3), 343–364.

Whittaker, J. (2020). Online radicalization and conspiracies. In S. M. Khasru (Ed.), *The digital age cyber space and social media: The challenges of security & radicalization* (pp. 129–150). The Institute for Policy Advocacy and Governance (IPAG).

Wojcieszak, M. (2008). False consensus goes online: Impact of ideologically homogeneous groups on false consensus. *Public Opinion Quarterly, 72*(4), 781–791. https://doi.org/10.1093/poq/nfn056

Wylde, A. (2020). Resilience revisited. In S. M. Khasru (Ed.), *The digital age, cyber space, and social media: The challenges of security & radicalization* (pp. 215–229). IPAG.

3

The Power of Participation: Methodology of the Pilot Study

Abstract This chapter outlines the methodology of the pilot study, designed to investigate how active content creation differs from passive consumption in its impact on confirmation bias. It details the research design, including the custom online environment where participants engaged with real-world articles. The pilot study's experimental setup, participant recruitment, and data analysis plan are discussed, offering initial insights into how active engagement can accelerate bias reinforcement. The findings inform adjustments for the main study, particularly in terms of how the study environment influences participant attitudes and behaviours.

Keywords Active content creation • Passive content creation • Content consumption • Polarization • Confirmation bias • Attitude of change • Online behaviour

3.1 Introduction of the Pilot Study Design: Active Vs. Passive Engagement in Content Consumption

This study sets out to explore how active content creation and immediate memory recall may reinforce preexisting beliefs through confirmation bias. Given the complexity of confirmation bias, which includes both selective information acquisition aligned with existing beliefs and potential reinforcement of these beliefs, this research aims to answer several key questions: Does active content creation strengthen individuals' convictions? How do memory retrieval and reinforcement influence confirmation bias? Additionally, by comparing passive and active engagement, this study seeks to reveal the relative impact of each mode on individuals' confirmation bias.

This chapter provides an in-depth look at data collection, analysis methods, and considerations for maintaining research validity, offering a detailed view of the study's rigorous approach to understanding online behaviour and the reinforcement of cognitive biases.

The pilot study served as a foundational step in designing the main study, helping refine the custom online environment, address participant recruitment challenges, and identify relevant variables. The feasibility assessment provided valuable insights that guided adjustments for the main study.

This section outlines the methodology, detailing the study's structure, participant recruitment, data analysis, and ethical considerations. Together, these elements form a comprehensive framework for examining the impact of active and passive memory recall on confirmation bias.

The pilot study's design includes a range of independent, dependent, mediating, and moderating variables:

Independent Variables: Political Attitude and Polarization Extremity
Dependent Variable: Confirmation Bias Search
Mediating Variable: Temporal Delay
Moderating variables: Active and passive content creation
Covariate Variable: Attitude of Change

Conducted within a custom-developed environment via R Studio and jspsych, the study presented participants with tasks involving headline selection and content creation. The participants' biases were assessed both before and after the intervention prompts. The design aligns with established research frameworks but was uniquely tailored to fit the specific demands of this study.

Several practical challenges arose, such as securing a suitable study host, which led to the study's placement in the University of Graz's computer lab and ensuring that ethical data handling was aligned with General Data Protection Regulation compliance. Recruitment poses its own difficulties, necessitating trials to establish reliable and credible participant data.

The intervention method chosen for the study addresses gaps in understanding the dynamics of confirmation bias, particularly within social media. The controlled study environment enabled a systematic investigation into the cognitive and social factors shaping confirmation bias and online engagement.

The study targeted a diverse group of US-based participants from various demographic backgrounds. Recruitment was facilitated through Amazon Mechanical Turk (MTurk), which provides a broader participant pool than typical student samples do.

The participants were required to have a high Human Intelligence Task (HIT) approval rate (over 90%) and were informed about data confidentiality and anonymity. The United States was selected because English-language articles and American media sources were used. The recruitment period spanned from late September to early December 2021, with participants compensated $3 per completed task.

The study employed convenience sampling via MTurk, allowing efficient participant recruitment while acknowledging limitations in broader generalizability. Eligibility criteria included an age minimum of 18, prior online work experience, and a baseline skill level. The study's description invited participants to share opinions on a social movement, using keywords such as "survey," "demographics," and "black lives matter." This approach ensured relevance to the study's objective while focusing on participants within the United States.

The participants completed tasks at an average of 26 minutes, with compensation verified through an autoapproval system. The recruitment process included informed consent, assurances of anonymity, and data security protocols, with data stored securely in text and CSV formats for compatibility with Statistical Package for the Social Sciences (SPSS). A final debrief provided an overview of the study's purpose and ethical practices.

The participants completed tasks across three blocks of BLM-related headlines, selecting a headline, reading the article, and either passively proceeding or actively creating content, depending on group assignment. The experimental group's prompts aimed to simulate feedback loops by introducing moments of active reflection or content creation, whereas the control group proceeded without these prompts.

This pilot study carefully addressed the intricacies of confirmation bias in the context of online engagement, exploring how active vs. passive engagement influences belief reinforcement. The subsequent chapters detail the research methodology and study procedures, laying the groundwork for the study's examination of temporal dynamics and cognitive bias in online environments.

3.2   Detailed Methodology, Including the Research Design, Sampling Procedures, and Custom Online Environment

In the data analysis phase, the study utilized a combination of FileZilla for secure data export and storage and SPSS and RStudio for robust statistical analysis. Ensuring data integrity was a priority, and a thorough data-cleaning process was implemented to maintain accuracy and consistency across all collected responses. This cleaning process specifically addressed free-response sections, particularly within the active storytelling tasks, where participants summarized the articles. These sections required closer inspection to filter out unrelated or nonsensical responses, thus preserving the reliability of participants' insights and avoiding any skewed analysis. Given the structured design of the questionnaire and the stringent participant vetting on Mechanical Turk, the data-cleaning needs were minimized, helping to ensure that the responses accurately reflected genuine participant engagement.

The research questions guiding this analysis were multidimensional, focusing on participants' perception shifts over time, the role of memory retrieval and coding in reinforcing confirmation bias, the influence of temporal dynamics, and the effects of different retrieval approaches across participant groups. To address these questions, an array of statistical techniques and correlations were employed to reveal patterns and insights into confirmation bias in digital engagement. The analysis included descriptive and inferential statistics to evaluate the relationships between variables, addressing how participants' attitudes and beliefs evolved in response to active versus passive engagement.

This methodology leverages both qualitative and quantitative insights, aligning with the study's objective to understand confirmation bias and its impact on online behaviour. By examining differences between active and passive content consumption modes, this study not only investigates the mechanics of cognitive bias but also considers its broader implications for societal attitudes and belief reinforcement.

The rigour of the analysis plan, supported by diverse statistical approaches, ensures that the study's findings are both valid and reliable. Through these methods, the study aims to offer meaningful contributions to the discipline by shedding light on the nuanced interplay between cognitive processes, memory dynamics, and confirmation bias in digital contexts, advancing our understanding of how these factors shape online interactions and belief formation.

3.3   Initial Findings on How Active Content Creation Affects Confirmation Bias Reinforcement

The pilot study was conducted to assess the effects of active commenting, memory retrieval, and selective exposure on confirmation bias within the context of a polarized social movement—Black Lives Matter (BLM). Specifically, this study aimed to investigate whether active content creation, coupled with immediate memory recall, influences individuals' preexisting beliefs and amplifies their viewpoints. Additionally, it explores the influence of temporal delays on selective exposure, examining both passive and active engagement to determine the relative strength of each in reinforcing confirmation bias.

This pilot study also evaluated whether a small sample size of $N = 20$ participants per group was adequate to detect significant effects or if modifications to the sample size, instrumentation, study design, and data analysis would be necessary to yield statistically meaningful results. The findings provided insights that informed these adjustments for the main study, ensuring that the research design was robust enough to capture the nuanced dynamics of confirmation bias reinforcement.

Initial findings revealed a noticeable effect on participants' attitudes, even within this limited sample size. However, these effects were not immediately discernible and required both descriptive analysis and advanced statistical techniques, including regression modelling and analysis in SPSS. By employing nonlinear least squares (NLS) modelling, which is effective for capturing U-shaped trends, this study explored the degree of attitude shifts among participants with varying levels of initial polarization. This approach allowed the study to focus on the magnitude of changes without bias towards the direction of change.

In the experimental group, participants with extreme initial polarization (either very positive or very negative views on BLM) exhibited minimal change in their attitudes, indicating a tendency to remain steadfast in their views. Conversely, those with more moderate attitudes displayed subtle shifts in opinion, suggesting that active commenting and memory retrieval might have prompted a degree of reflection that influenced their beliefs. This finding supports the hypothesis that individuals with less extreme positions are more susceptible to attitudinal shifts when engaging in reflective content creation, whereas those with strong preexisting biases tend to reinforce their viewpoints.

In the control group, the passive engagement protocol revealed similar trends, albeit with less pronounced effects. The participants who answered multiple-choice questions after reading each article (without active content creation) demonstrated minimal attitude change, indicating that passive consumption alone may not significantly alter established beliefs. Interestingly, both groups tended to select articles that aligned with their political affiliations—leaning towards either right-leaning, left-leaning, or neutral perspectives—reinforcing the confirmation bias phenomenon whereby individuals favour information that validates their preexisting beliefs.

The U-shaped curve, a key outcome of the NLS model, underscored a critical relationship between initial polarization and the extent of attitudinal shifts. This curve, fitted to the absolute values of the changes in BLM ratings and polarization levels, showed that participants with moderate initial attitudes were more likely to experience shifts, whereas those with extreme initial polarization remained anchored in their views. This trend was particularly visible in the control group, where the coefficients for the quadratic term suggested a stronger U-shaped pattern than in the experimental group. For the experimental group, the effect was subtler, indicating that active engagement may introduce a degree of reflection that could mitigate extreme polarization effects, although not to a statistically significant extent.

The study design included a pre-test and post-test survey assessing confirmation bias via a Likert scale ranging from 0 (most negative) to 10 (most positive). This scale facilitated the measurement of changes in attitudes towards BLM, focusing on participants' selective exposure and their degree of reflection. The pre-test scores provided a baseline for analysing the impact of content engagement on participants' attitudes. For the main analysis, absolute values of the changes in BLM ratings were computed to focus on the magnitude of change rather than direction, which allowed the detection of patterns indicative of confirmation bias.

In terms of statistical analysis, the R script used for the study computed absolute changes in BLM ratings and polarization levels (e.g. amount_of_change_abs, polarization_pre_abs, and polarization_post_abs). This script implemented a nonlinear model to capture U-shaped patterns, with findings visualized through regression models that demonstrated distinct trends in the control and experimental groups.

Figure 3.1 shows the fitted U-shaped equations for each group.

- **Control Group**: $y = -0.379x2 + 2.157x - 1.068y = -0.379x2 + 2.157x - 1.068$
- **Experimental Group**: $y = 0.009x2 - 0.374x + 2.036y = 0.009x2 - 0.374x + 2.036$

These curves illustrate how each group's attitudes towards BLM fluctuated across levels of polarization, with a more pronounced U shape in the control group. This distinction suggests that passive engagement may lead to a more consistent reinforcement of existing attitudes, whereas

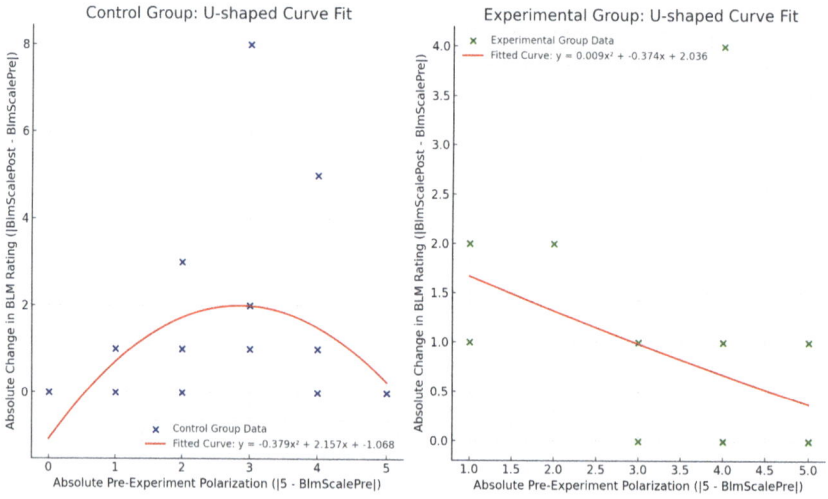

Fig. 3.1 Control group U-shaped curve fit (left), experimental group U-shaped curve fit (right). This figure presents the fitted U-shaped curves for both the control group (left) and the experimental group (right), based on the data collected during the study

active engagement, while less pronounced, allows for a modest degree of attitude shift among less polarized individuals.

Further analysis focused on the control group's passive content consumption and its impact on attitude change. For this group, the preexposure mean attitude score was 7.3, which decreased to 6.65 post exposure. This slight reduction was not statistically significant (p = 0.222), with a weak negative correlation (-0.159) between initial attitudes and the change in attitudes. Although weak, this correlation suggested that participants with initially positive attitudes might experience a slight decrease, but the relationship was insufficiently strong to support a definitive conclusion.

Similarly, for the experimental group, the preexposure mean was 6.25, decreasing to 5.95 post exposure, with a moderate negative correlation (-0.304) between initial attitudes and attitude changes. This correlation implied a tendency for participants with favourable views to display a slight decrease in attitudes after active engagement, although the effect size remained modest, and the p value indicated no statistical significance.

The pilot study also revealed that temporal delays had a minimal mitigating effect on confirmation bias in the control group, as the passive nature of multiple-choice questioning after each article did not encourage the critical reflection necessary to challenge existing biases. In contrast, the experimental group's active commenting task required participants to articulate their reflections, potentially introducing a reflective element that contributed to minor shifts in moderate attitudes.

Distribution plots of pre- and postexposure attitudes illustrated the spread and central tendencies of participant responses, reinforcing the statistical findings that confirmed minimal changes in polarization levels for both groups. These visualizations, alongside correlation analyses, provided a comprehensive overview of the relationship between initial attitudes and subsequent changes.

Finally, a critical aspect of the pilot study was the exploration of the recruitment, data collection, and data cleaning processes. Recruitment was conducted through Mechanical Turk to ensure that diverse samples reflected the general US population. Data cleaning focused on ensuring that participants' free-writing responses were relevant and coherent, especially in the experimental group, where active commenting was a key variable. Duplicate entries were removed to ensure accuracy, and the raw data were stored securely in FileZilla, with further statistical analysis carried out in SPSS and RStudio.

The pilot study findings underscore the resilience of established attitudes and the limited impact of passive content consumption on polarization. However, the slight shifts observed in the experimental group suggested that active engagement could prompt minor attitude adjustments, particularly among individuals with moderate attitudes. These insights informed the research design and methodology for the main study, emphasizing the importance of incorporating both passive and active engagement modes to understand the reinforcement of confirmation bias and the potential for challenging it within digital echo chambers.

In conclusion, the pilot study highlighted the complexities of confirmation bias reinforcement within a polarized online environment, where both passive and active engagement contribute differently to attitude formation and reinforcement. The observed U-shaped pattern in the control group underscored the stability of extreme attitudes, whereas the experimental group's responses indicated that active engagement may offer a pathway to modest attitude shifts among less polarized individuals. These findings laid the groundwork for the main study, guiding the development of a robust methodology that would further explore the interplay between selective exposure, confirmation bias, and the impact of active content creation on online attitudes and beliefs. The next chapter discusses the main study in detail, examining the effects of different engagement levels on attitude polarization and the nuances of confirmation bias in the context of digital media consumption.

Understanding the role of confirmation bias is essential for addressing the spread of conspiracy theories, misinformation, or radical beliefs. At their core, these beliefs thrive on the human tendency to seek information that aligns with preexisting worldviews, often at the expense of truth. Addressing this requires more than just presenting facts; it demands strategies that help individuals recognize and question their biases, fostering openness to alternative perspectives. By promoting critical thinking, encouraging thoughtful dialogue, and equipping people with tools to navigate the digital information landscape, we can weaken the grip of confirmation bias. Ultimately, combating conspiracy theories is not just about dismantling falsehoods but also about empowering individuals to approach information with curiosity, reflection, and a commitment to seeking truth over validation.

4

Deep Dive into Confirmation Bias: Experimental Insights

Abstract This chapter delves into the main study's experimental design and findings, offering a comprehensive analysis of how confirmation bias is reinforced in digital spaces. The results reveal significant differences between participants who actively create content and those who passively consume it, with active creators showing a faster reinforcement of bias. The role of temporal dynamics is also emphasized, demonstrating how time delays between content exposure and reflection amplify or moderate bias. The findings provide critical insights into the cognitive mechanisms underlying confirmation bias in digital environments and the role of user interaction in shaping beliefs.

Keywords Confirmation bias • Attitude change • Online environment • Polarization • Source affiliation • Temporal dynamics • News selection patterns

4.1   Detailed Analysis of the Main Study Methodology and Results

The main study focuses on exploring how confirmation bias and attitude change are influenced by active versus passive memory recall. Specifically, it aims to understand the factors that contribute to changes in attitude polarization and how confirmation bias is reinforced in online environments such as temporal dynamics or source affiliation.

This section presents a comprehensive methodology for examining how confirmation bias and attitude change are influenced by active versus passive memory recall. Through an intricate breakdown of the study's structure, data collection methods, participant recruitment, instrumentation, data analysis techniques, and ethical considerations, it offers an in-depth look at the systematic approach applied to explore the complex dynamics between cognitive biases and memory processes.

The study design incorporated various types of variables, including the following:

- **Independent Variables:**
  - Political Attitude
  - Polarization Extremity
- **Dependent Variables:**
  - Confirmation Bias Search
- **Mediating Variables:**
  - Temporal Delay
- **Moderating Variables:**
  - Active and Passive Content Creation
- **Covariate Variables**:
  - Attitude of change

The research employed an experimental design with two distinct phases—a pilot study followed by a comprehensive study. Both studies were executed within a custom-built online environment, specifically tailored to incorporate the study's diverse variables and logical components. Developed in RStudio and jspsych, this environment allows participants to engage in tasks ranging from passive checkbox selection to active content creation. The initial bias assessment of participants was followed by targeted intervention prompts, concluding with a re-evaluation. This method aligns with established experimental designs within the discipline, advancing the understanding of confirmation bias and selective exposure in online settings.

The custom-developed study environment was hosted on the University of Graz's computer lab server, necessitated by the unique data requirements and variable manipulations integral to the study's design. However, constraints related to GDPR compliance and data handling pose logistical challenges, which are managed through the use of FileZilla for secure data transfer and storage. Additionally, participant recruitment required multiple trial phases to source reliable data, ultimately refined through Mechanical Turk (MTurk), where participants were selected on the basis of HIT approval rates, ensuring credibility and consistency in responses.

The design of the intervention aimed to bridge existing gaps in understanding online confirmation bias and behaviour, particularly in social media contexts. By enabling controlled manipulation of variables within a custom environment, the study could comprehensively investigate the cognitive and social factors influencing confirmation bias.

The participants' ideological positions on the Black Lives Matter (BLM) movement were gauged via a Likert scale ranging from 0 (negative) to 10 (positive). This scale provided insight into the ideological spectrum within the sample, revealing diverse attitudes, with a slight tilt towards conservative perspectives, as indicated by headline selection tendencies.

The confirmation bias measurement examined participants' headline choices, evaluating the alignment between their political views and the tone of selected headlines (negative, positive, or neutral towards BLM). This approach revealed patterns in selective exposure, offering insights into how individuals engage with content that reinforces preexisting beliefs. The study further differentiated between active engagement (creating hypothetical "X" [formerly Twitter] comments) and passive engagement (responding to multiple-choice questions), allowing an analysis of how the interaction level impacts confirmation bias and polarization. Temporal dynamics varied between groups: while the control group encountered delays through multiple-choice questions, the experimental group faced biases during both content blocks and active reflection in written responses.

By operationalizing selective exposure through article choice, the study examined the role of content alignment with preexisting attitudes, exploring whether exposure to diverse views could prompt attitude shifts in those with initially extreme positions.

The recruitment methods for the target population mirrored those used in the pilot study, maintaining a consistent sampling framework.

Sampling procedures from the pilot study were applied directly to the main study, as they proved effective in meeting recruitment goals and ensuring data integrity.

Participant recruitment and data collection procedures, which were previously validated in the pilot study, were similarly employed in the main study. The participants were required to have a high HIT approval rating and a US-based location to ensure credibility.

The informed consent process included a full explanation of the study's objectives, methods, and data handling practices. Anonymity was maintained, with no personal identifiers collected, and all the data were securely stored on password-protected servers. The participants exited the study with a debrief, outlining the study's purpose, emphasizing confidentiality, and providing contact information for further questions. This process ensured that the participants were fully informed, with all the data handled ethically and securely.

Building on pilot study insights, the main study expanded the sample to 80 participants and introduced additional variables:

- **Disclosure of Headline Sources**: Headlines were now attributed to sources such as CNN, Reuters, and Fox News.
- **Memory Prompts**: Both groups received memory prompts, with the control group using multiple-choice questions and the experimental group engaging in active content creation.

The primary research question investigated factors influencing attitude polarization and confirmation bias within an online setting. This was complemented by inquiries into whether highly polarized participants would maintain strong biases, even when confronted with contrasting headlines (disclosed by news source affiliation). To enhance group comparability, passive memory prompts were added to the control group, although only the experimental group participated in active content creation.

Hypotheses:

- **Main Hypothesis**: Active content consumption (comment creation) results in a stronger confirmation search than does passive consumption, especially when headline sources are disclosed.
- **Sub-Hypotheses**:

  1. Active engagement via content creation is associated with heightened confirmation bias.
  2. Passive content consumption, with minimal interaction, has a lesser impact on reinforcing bias.
  3. The interplay of the content consumption mode and temporal delay, moderated by headline sources, affects confirmation bias.

- **Null Hypothesis**: There is no significant difference in confirmation bias intensity between active and passive consumers, despite headline source disclosure.

Data analysis relied on FileZilla for data export, with SPSS and R Studio used for statistical evaluation (detailed in Appendix II). Data cleaning ensured accuracy by eliminating duplicate entries and unrelated responses, particularly in active content creation, where participants summarized articles. The structured questionnaire minimized the need for extensive data cleaning, given MTurk's recruitment quality.

The key research questions centred on conflict perception over time, the influence of memory retrieval on confirmation bias, temporal dynamics, and the impact of active versus passive retrieval methods. Statistical techniques, including descriptive and advanced analyses, address these questions and validate the study objectives.

The study environment and methodological framework transitioned seamlessly from pilot to main study, with refinements in headline source disclosure (Fig. 4.1) and memory prompts for the control group (Fig. 4.2). This custom interface, developed in jspsych and R Studio, allows precise variable manipulation.

Upon entry, the participants encountered a welcome screen, a brief introduction to the BLM movement, and a data privacy notice. A demographic questionnaire covered age, gender, political affiliation, and voting eligibility. The participants then completed a pre-test Likert scale assessment of BLM attitudes before choosing between right-leaning, left-leaning, and neutral headlines, followed by content engagement specific to their group assignment (either passive or active).

For the control group, each content block involved reading headlines, followed by multiple-choice questions. The experimental group, by contrast, actively created mock comments, allowing for in-depth analysis of how reflective engagement affects confirmation bias.

The intervention was executed as planned. Articles on BLM were provided, with participants assigned to control or experimental conditions. The control group participants passively consumed content, whereas the

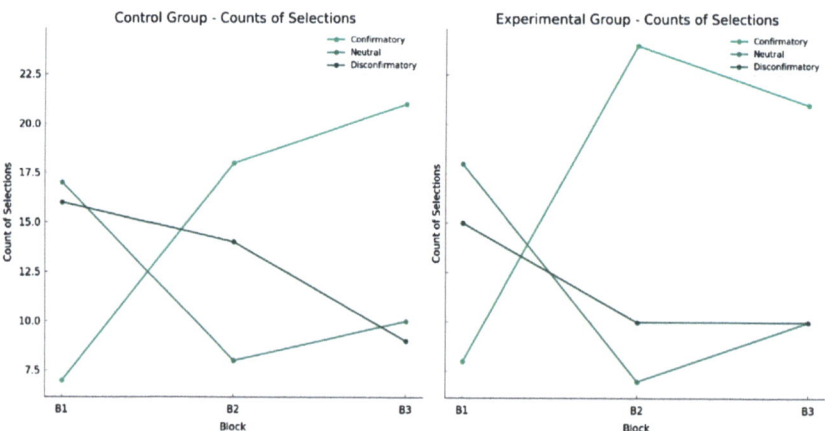

Fig. 4.1 Confirmatory search control group (left) and experimental group (right). This figure presents the search behaviour of the control group (left) and the experimental group (right), highlighting differences in confirmatory search patterns

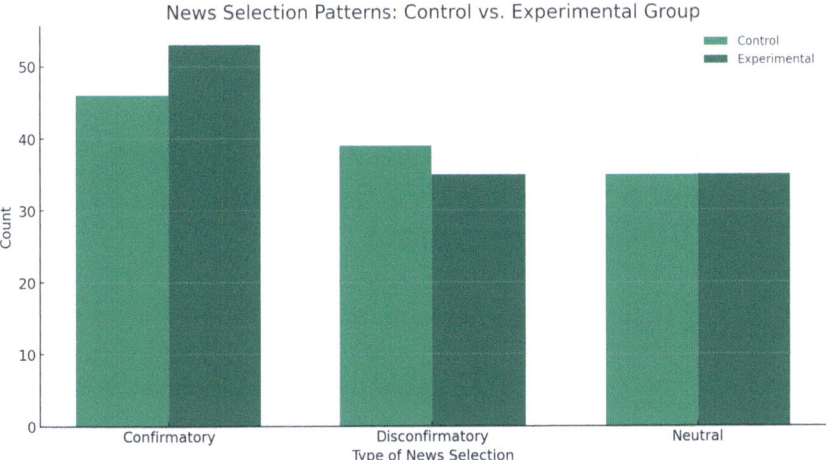

Fig. 4.2 News selection patterns, control vs. experimental group. This figure illustrates the differences in news selection patterns between the control group and the experimental group, comparing tendencies towards confirmatory, disconfirmatory, and neutral news articles

experimental group engaged in content creation. The treatment closely adhered to the study design, with both groups consistently accessing content and tasks without issues.

The intervention resulted in no adverse events or ethical challenges. The participants completed the tasks without experiencing harm or discomfort, aligning with the ethical standards established to protect their well-being.

The main study's methodological rigour, grounded in the pilot study findings, enhanced the reliability of the outcomes by refining recruitment, data collection, and environmental design. The introduction of disclosed headline sources, combined with active and passive memory prompts, facilitated a nuanced exploration of confirmation bias and attitude polarization within a polarized social context. Through a comprehensive, ethically grounded research design, this study extends the knowledge on the relationships among selective exposure, memory retrieval, and confirmation bias in digital environments. The subsequent sections analyse these findings in depth and examine their statistical parameters, correlations, and broader implications for our understanding of cognitive biases in online spaces.

4.2   Comparison Between Active Content Creators and Passive Consumers in Terms of Bias Reinforcement

This section examines how active content creators—those engaged in producing responses, comments, or summaries—compared with passive consumers, who primarily read and answer multiple-choice questions, reinforce confirmation bias. By investigating both groups' tendencies towards confirmatory news selection and changes in attitudes, we aim to understand how different engagement levels influence the reinforcement of existing beliefs. The analysis explores whether active creation accelerates bias reinforcement or prompts critical reflection, contrasting it with the effects of passive consumption on bias maintenance over time.

This study illuminates the intricate relationships among confirmation bias, attitude change, and engagement levels within digital environments. The findings suggest that while active engagement through content creation fosters greater involvement and accelerates belief reinforcement, it does not necessarily mitigate confirmation bias. Both the active and the passive engagement modes support the reinforcement of existing beliefs over time, with temporal dynamics influencing how rapidly this reinforcement unfolds. Notably, the experimental group's negative correlation between initial attitudes and attitude change suggests that active engagement may encourage some moderation of views. These insights offer valuable directions for strategies aimed at addressing confirmation bias and fostering more balanced perspectives in digital media consumption. Future research could explore factors such as source credibility and the role of timing in interventions designed to reduce bias and promote critical thinking.

The primary objective of the main study was to expand upon the pilot study findings by examining how selective search, content creation, and information recall impact attitude change and confirmation bias. With a larger sample of 80 participants, the main study provided a more comprehensive analysis of how exposure to information shapes individual attitudes and the extent to which active content creation influences this process. This study collected data through a custom online environment and analysed them via Python libraries such as Pandas, Matplotlib, and Seaborn (Appendix G provides details).

The study effectively managed the complexities of data collection, participant recruitment, ethical considerations, and experimental manipulation, allowing for a robust exploration of how active storytelling influences confirmation bias. With this foundation, the subsequent sections will detail the study's results, examining the connections between cognitive processes and belief reinforcement.

The main hypothesis posited a significant difference in confirmation bias intensity between participants engaged in active content consumption and those engaged in passive content consumption, particularly with respect to news source disclosure. Analysis of news selection patterns revealed that both the active and the passive groups demonstrated strong confirmatory news selection tendencies, see Fig. 4.1, suggesting that engagement type did not drastically reduce confirmation bias. While active engagement might involve heightened involvement and critical thinking, it does not necessarily lower confirmation bias, especially when headline source disclosure is considered. Temporal dynamics further emphasized this effect, as both groups showed an increase in confirmatory search over time. Notably, the experimental group, which was tasked with active engagement through content creation, reached peak confirmatory search at a faster rate, as shown in Fig. 4.4.

Sub-Hypothesis 1: This hypothesis suggests that active content consumption amplifies confirmation bias due to greater engagement with information. However, the experimental group exhibited a similar degree of confirmation bias as the control group did, implying that while active engagement through content creation fosters deeper interaction with the material, it may also reinforce preexisting biases.

Sub-Hypothesis 2: Passive content consumption is hypothesized to reinforce confirmation bias by reducing exposure to contradictory perspectives. The results supported this to an extent, as the control group showed a pattern of news selection that aligned with the experimental group, indicating that both active and passive consumption perpetuate confirmation bias—through limited engagement in the former and reinforcement of existing views during content creation in the latter.

Sub-Hypothesis 3: This hypothesis proposes that consumption mode effects on confirmation bias are moderated by temporal delay and source credibility. While direct analysis focused on active versus passive consumption, the results suggested that factors such as source credibility play a substantial role in shaping confirmation bias. The observed similarity in confirmation bias intensity across groups points to the moderating influence of factors beyond the engagement mode alone, with timing and source credibility critical in understanding confirmation bias in digital consumption.

The research question concerning the relationship between polarization strength and opinion change was not supported as expected. Analysis revealed a significant negative correlation in the experimental group, where participants with initially more positive BLM attitudes tended to decrease scores postexposure, whereas those with lower scores tended to increase. This moderation trend, observed only in the experimental group, suggests a nuanced relationship between engagement type and confirmation bias.

- Control Group: $r = 0.033$, $p = 0.842$ (nonsignificant correlation).
- Experimental Group: $r = -0.535$, $p < 0.001$ (significant negative correlation).

The results suggest that content creation and active engagement influence confirmation bias by fostering a preference for confirmatory news, with this effect becoming more pronounced in later stages of the experiment. As the experimental group actively created content, the participants displayed greater confirmatory news selection tendencies than did the control group did, which aligned with the expectation that engagement could reinforce confirmation bias.

The correlation analysis further demonstrated that participants in the experimental group showed a pronounced shift towards confirmatory search as the experiment progressed, supporting the hypothesis that active engagement reinforces existing biases. In contrast, the control group's temporal delay through multiple-choice questions did not measurably affect their search speed.

The experimental group analysis focused on key metrics:

1. BLM scale score change: Calculated by assessing pre- and postexposure score differences, testing for significant shifts.
2. Confirmation Bias in News Selection: Analysed participants' patterns in confirmatory versus disconfirmatory news selection across experiment blocks.
3. Correlation Analysis: Investigated the relationship between initial BLM scores and postexposure changes.

The BLM score change analysis of the experimental group revealed the following:

- The mean change is ~0.07, indicating a slight average increase.
- The standard deviation was 1.40, suggesting variability.
- Range: –3-+7, with a median of 0.

A paired t test (p = 0.74) indicated that changes in BLM scale scores before and after exposure were not statistically significant. Similarly, news selection patterns showed an increase in confirmatory news preferences over time, highlighting participants' tendency to seek information that aligned with preexisting attitudes.

The correlation analysis revealed a significant negative relationship between initial BLM scores and extent of change:

- Correlation coefficient: r = -0.535, p = 0.0003.

This suggests a trend towards moderation, with participants adjusting views towards a more neutral position when exposed to information aligned with their biases.

Figures 4.1, 4.2 and 4.3 illustrate the findings for the experimental group, including the distribution of BLM scale score changes, news selection tendencies across blocks, and correlations between initial scores and postexposure changes.

For the control group, similar analyses were conducted:

- BLM scale score change: This indicates a slight decrease on average (-0.025).
- News Selection: This group showed an increase in confirmatory news selection over time, similar to the experimental group.
- Correlation analysis revealed no significant relationship between initial BLM scores and changes (r = 0.033, p = 0.842).

When both groups were compared:

- Attitude change: The experimental group showed a slight positive shift, and the control group showed a slight decrease.
- News Selection Patterns: Both groups showed a preference for confirmatory news, with a greater tendency in the experimental group.
- Initial scores and changes: The experimental group presented a moderate negative correlation, and the control group presented a very weak correlation.

Figure 4.2 visualizes news selection patterns across groups, Fig. 4.3 compares attitude shifts, and Fig. 4.4 highlights initial score and postexposure change correlations.

To compare the experimental group of active content creators with the control group of passive consumers effectively, the focus is on key aspects of bias reinforcement:

- **Attitude Change**: Active content creators, or those engaged in content creation, showed a slight positive shift in attitudes towards the BLM movement, whereas passive consumers exhibited a slight negative shift. However, the direction and magnitude of these shifts highlight differing impacts on bias reinforcement.
- **News Selection Patterns**: Both active creators and passive consumers demonstrated confirmatory news selection over time, with active creators displaying a slightly greater tendency for confirmatory news. This

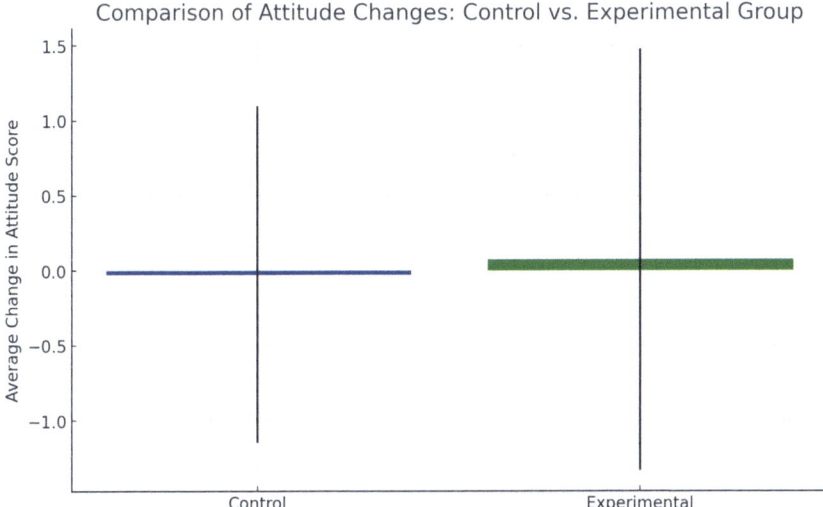

Fig. 4.3 Comparison of attitude changes between the control and experimental groups. This figure compares the changes in attitudes towards the BLM movement between the control and experimental groups, highlighting the differences in the magnitude and direction of attitude shifts post exposure

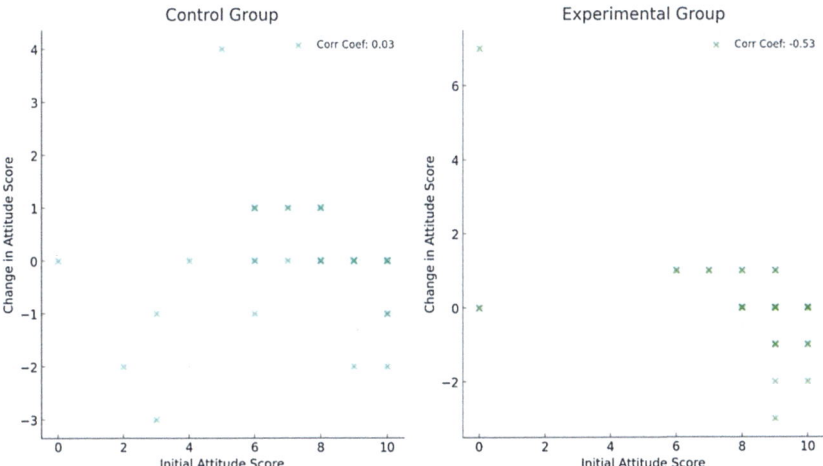

Fig. 4.4 Correlation between initial attitudes and changes post exposure. This figure illustrates the correlation between participants' initial attitudes towards the BLM movement and the changes in those attitudes after exposure to experimental content

pattern suggests that both engagement levels reinforce biases but may do so through different mechanisms, with active engagement potentially increasing the tendency to select confirmatory information.

- **Correlation between Initial Scores and Changes**: For active content creators, there was a moderate negative correlation between initial BLM scores and attitude change, suggesting that actively engaging with content might encourage some moderation of extreme views. In contrast, passive consumers showed a very weak correlation, implying that passive engagement alone does little to alter deeply held beliefs.

This research provides valuable insights into how information search, content creation, and attitude polarization interact in online environments. Key findings include the following:

- Polarization and Opinion Change: Less polarized individuals showed greater opinion shifts after exposure, suggesting that moderates may be more open to change.
- Content Creation Influence: Active content creation reinforced preexisting beliefs, potentially limiting openness to contrasting information.
- Temporal Dynamics and Confirmation Bias: Both groups showed increased confirmatory search over time, with the experimental group reaching this point faster, emphasizing active engagement's role in strengthening biases.
- Attitude strength and change correlation: The experimental group displayed a significant negative correlation between initial attitude strength and postexposure change, indicating that content creation might lessen the impact of new information on established attitudes.

These findings advance the understanding of confirmation bias within online environments, revealing how selective exposure and active content creation reinforce cognitive biases. Future work could explore strategies to counter selective exposure, foster critical thinking and reduce polarization. The subsequent chapter will discuss these implications in detail, offering potential applications and strategies for addressing confirmation bias in the digital age.

4.3   Key Insights into How Temporal Dynamics (Delays in Content Exposure) Influence Confirmation Bias

Temporal dynamics—the timing and delay in content exposure—play a critical role in the development and reinforcement of confirmation bias. This study's design, particularly with the inclusion of temporal delays, allows for a unique investigation into how the timing of information encounters influences selective exposure and the intensification of existing beliefs. By comparing active content creators with passive consumers, we can identify distinct patterns that highlight how temporal delays impact each group's confirmation bias differently.

In both groups, temporal delays were integrated to create varying levels of immediacy in participants' responses. For the experimental group, which engaged in active content creation, the responses were immediate: the participants were prompted to draft summaries or comments immediately after each content block. In contrast, the control group faced a slight temporal delay in content reinforcement, with multiple-choice questions interspersed between content exposures. This structure allowed us to observe how temporal spacing affects confirmation bias when participants either actively engage with content or passively consume it.

1. **Accelerated Confirmation Bias in Active Content Creators**

    One of the main insights from the study is that active content creators experience faster reinforcement of confirmation bias due to the immediate processing of information. Without the temporal delay imposed in the control group, the experimental group engaged in rapid opinion reinforcement. Each interaction—prompted by content creation tasks—allows participants to process and reiterate their initial beliefs, creating a self-reinforcing loop. As they expressed their reactions through comments, participants not only solidified their attitudes but also strengthened selective exposure, tending towards information that aligned with their preexisting biases at an accelerated rate.

2. **Delayed Confirmation Bias Development in Passive Consumers**

In contrast, the control group, which experienced temporal delays through structured multiple-choice questions, exhibited a slower development of confirmation bias. The multiple-choice format did not prompt active content creation and thus reduced the immediacy of emotional engagement with the material. This delay allowed for some degree of cognitive detachment, and while participants still gravitated towards confirmatory information over time, they did so at a slower pace. This finding indicates that temporal delays can moderate the reinforcement of confirmation bias, especially when engagement remains passive and detached from immediate content production.

3. **Temporal Influence on Selective Exposure and Cognitive Flexibility**

Temporal delays also appeared to influence cognitive flexibility, or the openness to engage with contrasting perspectives. For example, the control group, subjected to multiple-choice prompts after each content block, exhibited a more measured engagement pattern and occasionally explored neutral or disconfirming content. This contrasted with the experimental group's pattern of sustained confirmatory selection. The findings suggest that introducing temporal delays between content exposure and participant response can create a cognitive "breathing room," potentially reducing the intensity of confirmation bias. Passive engagement with built-in delays may thus allow for more reflective consumption of information rather than immediate bias reinforcement.

4. **Temporal Dynamics and Moderation of Extreme Views**

Another notable insight is how temporal delays influence the potential moderation of extreme views. In the experimental group, the absence of delay often resulted in quick convergence towards confirmatory beliefs, whereas the control group displayed a gradual shift towards moderation. This was particularly evident in the tendency for initially polarized participants in the control group to move slightly towards a more neutral position postexposure. The delay introduced by multiple-choice questions allowed these participants to reflect on their initial biases without the immediacy of content creation, suggesting that well-timed delays can contribute to a softening of extreme views in online engagement contexts.

5. **Impact of Temporal Dynamics on Sustained Bias over Multiple Exposures**

   Over the course of the study, temporal dynamics appeared to influence the persistence of confirmation bias. Both groups showed increased selective exposure across content blocks, but the experimental group's rate of bias reinforcement was more immediate, reaching higher levels of confirmatory behaviour in the second block. In contrast, the control group required the entire study duration to exhibit similar levels of selection bias. This difference underscores the role of temporal delays in either sustaining or intensifying confirmation bias, suggesting that strategic use of delays could temper the speed and extent of biased information consumption.

Temporal dynamics play a crucial role in understanding how artificial intelligence influences opinion polarization through selective exposure and network interactions. Bhalla et al. (2021) explore how time-dependent factors, such as evolving local edge dynamics and friend-of-friend link recommendations, shape opinion networks. Using the Friedkin–Johnsen opinion dynamics model, their study demonstrated how the temporal development of connections within a network contributes to polarization by reinforcing confirmation bias and limiting exposure to diverse viewpoints. Friend-of-friend recommendations, driven by AI algorithms, accelerate the creation of tightly knit clusters within networks, which further entrench shared opinions and reduce opportunities for cross-ideological interactions. These dynamics highlight how AI's influence on social networks not only perpetuates but also amplifies polarization over time, emphasizing the need for a deeper understanding of the temporal aspects of opinion formation to address the reinforcing effects of biased information. The findings on temporal dynamics open avenues for deeper exploration into how digital media platforms might apply controlled delays to reduce the impact of confirmation bias in online environments. For example, introducing time-based breaks in content feeds or creating "pause points" that delay user reactions could encourage more reflective processing. These interventions could be particularly effective in environments prone to echo chambers or where engagement is emotionally charged. Additionally, incorporating temporal delays could counteract the effects of algorithmic curation, which intensifies exposure to biased content, promoting a more balanced and less immediate consumption of information.

Ultimately, temporal dynamics emerge as a key factor in understanding and potentially mitigating confirmation bias. While both active and passive consumers tend towards selective exposure, the timing of their engagement significantly shapes the depth and speed of bias reinforcement. Given the increasingly fast-paced and immediate nature of online media, these findings suggest that building intentional temporal breaks into digital content delivery could foster critical thinking and reduce susceptibility to biased reinforcement over time.

Reference

Bhalla, N., Lechowicz, A., & Musco, C. (2021). Local edge dynamics and opinion polarization. In *Proceedings of the sixteenth ACM international conference on web search and data mining* (pp. 6–14). Association for Computing Machinery.

5

Bridging Findings and Future Directions: A Comprehensive Discussion

Abstract In this concluding chapter, the book synthesizes the findings from both the pilot and main studies, offering a combined analysis of how confirmation bias operates in digital environments. The discussion covers the study's limitations, threats to validity, and the broader implications for digital media platforms. It also provides practical recommendations for mitigating the negative effects of confirmation bias, such as promoting critical thinking and diversifying content exposure. The chapter ends with suggestions for future research on the intersection of cognitive biases, digital engagement, and social media, and how these insights can inform both policy and platform design.

Keywords Confirmation bias • Conspiracy theory • Polarization • Critical thinking • Misinformation • Cognitive biases • Media literacy • Digital literacy

5.1 Combined Analysis of the Pilot and Main Study Results and Broader Implications for Digital Environments

In the age of ubiquitous digital connectivity, the ways in which individuals select, consume, and disseminate information have transformed the very fabric of social discourse. This chapter bridges the findings from both the pilot and main studies, integrating insights into how confirmation bias, polarization, and selective exposure operate within digital environments. At the heart of this analysis lies the self-reinforcing cycle of confirmation bias, an essential driver of the echo chambers that characterize contemporary media landscapes. This feedback loop, where individuals seek out information that aligns with their preexisting beliefs, perpetuates polarization and restricts exposure to diverse perspectives.

This research, positioned at the intersection of psychology, digital media studies, and social dynamics, delves into the underlying mechanisms that fuel confirmation bias in both content consumption and creation. While confirmation bias is a well-established cognitive phenomenon, the accelerated spread of digital platforms has heightened its impact, reshaping societal interactions and amplifying the division between ideological groups. Individuals, now exposed primarily to information that confirms their beliefs, are immersed in echo chambers that become self-sustaining. This cycle leads to a narrowing of perspectives and reduces the likelihood of critical engagement with opposing viewpoints. The increasing prevalence of these echo chambers underscores the urgency of investigating how both active engagement with content (such as writing comments or creating posts) and passive consumption (such as browsing articles or scrolling through feeds) impact users' biases.

Our findings align with and extend the insights provided by Bergerot et al. (2024) regarding the role of confirmation bias in shaping decision-making processes. While Bergerot et al. demonstrated the potential benefits of moderate confirmation bias in controlled collective decision-making scenarios, our research highlights the challenges posed by active engagement in digital environments. Specifically, we observed that active engagement—such as content creation or immediate interaction with selected information—amplifies confirmation bias, leading to more entrenched attitudes and accelerated confirmatory information processing. Unlike the controlled agent-based settings studied by Bergerot et al., the dynamics of active engagement in real-world contexts appear to heighten the risks of polarization and reduce opportunities for balanced decision-making. This divergence underscores the importance of addressing confirmation bias at the individual level, particularly in environments shaped by algorithmic filtering and selective exposure. Our results suggest that while moderate bias may stabilize decision-making in collective artificial systems, its amplification through active engagement poses significant risks in digital ecosystems.

To counter the harmful effects of technology-related conspiracy beliefs and their broader implications, disrupting the feedback loops that reinforce them is crucial. Trang et al. (2024) emphasized the need for interventions targeting the perceptions of technology and its providers, which contributed to the proliferation of conspiracy mindsets. Building on this, our research suggests a two-pronged approach: first, promoting individual-level strategies such as critical thinking education and media literacy to reduce the impact of confirmation bias; second, implementing systemic changes to algorithmic curation that prioritize diverse perspectives over ideologically reinforcing content. Policymakers and technology designers must collaborate to develop tools and frameworks that minimize exposure to conspiracy-promoting content while fostering environments that encourage constructive dialogue and cross-ideological interactions. Addressing these challenges holistically can mitigate the social and cognitive impacts of conspiracy mindsets, enabling greater societal resilience in the face of crises.

The pilot study provided an initial glimpse into the effects of active content creation and memory recall on confirmation bias, particularly within the context of a polarized social movement, Black Lives Matter (BLM). By examining how individuals selected and responded to articles, the pilot study aimed to assess whether actively engaging with content, as opposed to passively consuming it, would lead to more pronounced biases. The participants' attitudes were measured both before and after exposure, with the experimental group encouraged to summarize their impressions, whereas the control group engaged in passive activities such as multiple-choice questions.

Building on the pilot study's preliminary insights, the main study introduced additional variables, including the source disclosure of articles, which indicated news outlets with recognizable ideological leanings. Expanding to a larger sample, the main study aimed to test whether active engagement through content creation significantly intensified participants' selective exposure and reinforcement of existing beliefs or whether passive browsing led to similar outcomes. Together, these studies reveal nuanced differences in how confirmation bias develops and persists in the digital realm.

One of the central findings from both studies is that confirmation bias persists in both active and passive engagement modes, although each influences the speed and depth of reinforcement differently. In the pilot study, active participants who generated comments after each article exhibited faster bias reinforcement than did those in the passive control group. This rapid reinforcement aligns with the tendency of active engagement to deepen personal involvement with the content, leading individuals to anchor their beliefs more firmly with each exposure.

In the main study, this trend continued, with the experimental group showing accelerated confirmation bias due to immediate engagement with content creation, suggesting that active engagement strengthens one's adherence to preexisting beliefs. However, even passive engagement reinforced confirmation bias over time, indicating that mere exposure to confirmatory information, without active processing, still sustains bias, albeit at a slower pace. This finding suggests that both active and passive content consumption modes contribute to confirmation bias in distinct ways, underscoring the pervasiveness of the bias across different forms of digital interaction.

Temporal dynamics—the timing between content exposures and responses—emerged as a critical factor in the reinforcement of confirmation bias. In both studies, active participants exhibited quicker shifts towards confirmatory behaviour, likely due to the immediacy of their responses, which did not allow time for reflection or alternative consideration. In the main study, passive participants, facing delays through multiple-choice prompts, demonstrated a slower reinforcement of bias.

This delay allowed for more moderated engagement, suggesting that pauses between content exposures might mitigate rapid bias reinforcement. This insight implies that strategically placed temporal breaks in digital environments could reduce the speed at which individuals reinforce their biases, potentially encouraging more balanced content interactions.

Both studies highlighted the moderating effect of attitude extremity on bias reinforcement. Participants with extreme initial attitudes towards the BLM movement demonstrated lower shifts in their opinions, remaining steadfast in their perspectives despite content exposure. In contrast, those with moderate initial views were more likely to exhibit attitude shifts post exposure, particularly in the experimental group. This outcome underscores that highly polarized individuals may be less susceptible to external influences that could alter their views, whereas those with more flexible positions may experience opinion shifts. These findings have significant implications for digital platforms, suggesting that interventions targeting moderately polarized users may have greater potential to promote balanced perspectives than efforts aimed at the most extreme groups.

An additional variable in the main study was source disclosure, which provided participants with cues about the ideological orientation of news outlets (e.g. CNN, Fox News). This factor influenced participants' content selection, particularly among those already inclined towards specific viewpoints. For example, participants often select articles from sources that are aligned with their political leanings, reinforcing their preexisting biases. This outcome illustrates the importance of source credibility and familiarity in digital media, as users tend to trust and select information from sources they perceive as ideologically compatible. Recognizing this pattern, digital platforms could benefit from emphasizing source diversity to expose users to a wider range of perspectives.

The act of actively creating content, as opposed to passively consuming it, proved to be a significant catalyst for confirmation bias reinforcement. In the main study, participants who engaged in content creation demonstrated higher levels of selective exposure, choosing confirmatory information more frequently as they progressed through the study. This trend suggests that the process of articulating and sharing one's views intensifies the selective attention given to confirming information, which in turn reinforces prior beliefs. These findings highlight the active role that users play in shaping their biases within digital environments, especially through content creation, which inherently prompts users to reflect on and reassert their beliefs.

The combined findings from the pilot and main studies underscore the complex and self-sustaining nature of confirmation bias in digital environments. Both active and passive forms of engagement perpetuate bias, albeit through different mechanisms, and temporal dynamics significantly shape how rapidly this reinforcement occurs. In this context, digital platforms face a growing need to address these reinforcing loops of bias, as they can contribute to societal polarization and limit exposure to diverse viewpoints.

1. **Designing for Temporal Delay and Balanced Exposure**

   Digital platforms could implement temporal delays between related content exposures or user interactions, creating a moment for reflection that could counteract rapid bias reinforcement. For example, staggered content feeds or scheduled interactions may slow down the immediate reinforcement of beliefs, potentially encouraging users to consider alternative perspectives.

2. **Integrating Source Diversity and Counterperspectives**

   By providing more diverse sources and promoting balanced exposure, platforms can mitigate echo chamber effects. The findings indicate that users gravitate towards familiar sources that align with their beliefs, but structured exposure to counterperspectives—perhaps through recommendation algorithms—could encourage a more holistic understanding of issues.

3. **Encouraging Passive Engagement and Reflection Opportunities**

   While active content creation intensifies bias reinforcement, passive consumption paired with reflective prompts can serve as a moderation tool. Implementing interactive elements that encourage passive users to consider different angles of an issue could foster critical thinking without reinforcing biases as strongly as direct content creation does.

4. **Personalizing Content Based on Attitude Extremity**

For highly polarized users, targeted interventions that encourage balanced exposure could be less effective. Instead, personalized content that gradually introduces various viewpoints, aligned with moderate users' preferences, may lead to more significant shifts. By focusing on users with flexible attitudes, platforms may be more successful in promoting open-mindedness and reducing polarization.

In summary, the findings from this research reveal that confirmation bias operates through complex interactions between the engagement mode, temporal dynamics, source credibility, and initial attitude extremity. Both active and passive users in digital environments tend towards selective exposure, but active engagement through content creation catalyses faster bias reinforcement. Temporal delays have emerged as a potentially valuable tool for mitigating this process, highlighting the significance of timing in digital interactions.

These insights underscore the potential for digital platforms to implement strategic design choices that counteract confirmation bias. In an era where echo chambers and polarized discourse threaten constructive societal interactions, understanding and addressing the mechanics of bias reinforcement can foster a more balanced, informed, and reflective digital ecosystem. This study illuminates the pathways through which individuals reinforce their beliefs online and offers directions for future research on designing more inclusive, diverse, and balanced digital spaces.

This study has significant implications across multiple dimensions, fostering positive social change through its contributions to theory and practice and addressing open questions in the literature. By comparing the pilot and main study results, this analysis delves into the nuanced ways in which confirmation bias manifests within digital environments, specifically through mechanisms of active content creation, passive content consumption, and temporal dynamics.

This study advances the theoretical understanding by exploring the intricate interplay among the components of confirmation bias, the differing impacts of active versus passive content consumption, and the influence of temporal delays in content exposure. Although the effects of confirmation bias have been extensively studied, the complex relationships among these factors remain underexplored. This research addresses that gap by focusing on the role of content creation as a mechanism that may intensify individuals' opinions and reveals how temporal delays shape the reinforcement of these beliefs. By analysing the process of content creation within controlled digital contexts, the study builds upon and enriches existing theoretical frameworks. Specifically, it contributes to the conceptual understanding of how confirmation bias is reinforced or, in certain cases, mitigated through varying degrees of engagement and timing of information retrieval.

Rather than seeking to reinvent current practices in the study of confirmation bias, this research enhances existing models by introducing newer elements, namely, active content creation and temporal dynamics, that influence belief formation. By identifying the unique impacts of engagement modes and the timing of content exposure on confirmation bias, this study offers valuable insights for practitioners, from content creators and digital media strategists to educators and digital platform designers. For instance, these findings suggest that content creators might consider implementing temporal delays or designing prompts that encourage diverse engagement patterns to foster open-mindedness and mitigate bias. Educators and platform developers could likewise apply these findings, informing the design of interfaces and engagement tools to balance perspectives and reduce polarization within digital environments. Through these insights, this study bridges the gap between theoretical exploration and practical applications, translating complex concepts into actionable recommendations for digital media environments.

The research also fills a significant gap in the literature by exploring the intersection of confirmation bias, memory retrieval through content creation, and temporal dynamics within the context of digital content consumption. Although confirmation bias has been extensively examined, limited research has addressed the nuanced relationships among these factors in a contemporary digital setting, particularly within the context of social movements. By examining how these elements converge and interact, this study provides a more comprehensive understanding of how digital engagement, whether passive or active, shapes opinion formation and sustains confirmation bias. Moreover, the study's focus on the Black

Lives Matter movement as a case for this analysis illuminates the potential for digital platforms to play a role in shaping and reinforcing public sentiment on contentious social issues. This study's integration of real-world social movement content reinforces its relevance, underscoring how individuals' engagement with digital media can affect belief formation at the societal level.

The implications extend beyond theoretical advancement to encompass practical insights and further address a gap in the literature. By shedding light on the role of content creation and temporal dynamics in reinforcing confirmation bias, particularly within the context of highly polarized issues such as social movements, this research sets the stage for broader implications in digital media. The findings indicate that the timing of information retrieval—such as when users are prompted to create content or reflect on prior exposure—can significantly influence whether individuals are open to diverse perspectives or instead become further entrenched in their views. Such insights may contribute to strategies for fostering more balanced information ecosystems and promoting critical thinking in digital interactions.

While confirmation bias and selective exposure have been previously studied in digital contexts, this research introduces a new angle by investigating the dynamics of temporal effects and active content creation. By examining the connection between content creation and bias reinforcement, particularly in cases where users are prompted to select information aligned with their preexisting views, this study offers a novel perspective. This approach enabled participants to engage with news articles about the Black Lives Matter movement in an online environment specifically crafted for the study. The participants were either asked to actively respond by creating content (such as simulated tweets) or to passively engage with content through multiple-choice tasks, allowing a comparison of how these differing modes of engagement impacted confirmation bias.

The results aligned with the study's hypotheses, showing meaningful differences in how passive versus active engagement influenced participants' levels of confirmation bias. Notably, the study revealed that active engagement, especially when paired with immediate retrieval tasks, reinforced confirmation bias more rapidly than did passive engagement. This pattern underscores the potential for active content creation to contribute to the intensification of existing biases, especially in highly charged topics such as social justice and political issues. These findings reinforce the need for further research to investigate the implications of active engagement in online environments and how this mode of interaction may contribute to echo chambers.

Through a comprehensive examination of engagement types and timing, this study contributes to a robust understanding of the factors that reinforce or mitigate confirmation bias in digital environments. Presenting both established knowledge and emerging insights offers a foundation for future research to expand on these dynamics, ideally applying these findings within real-world digital platforms. This line of research opens avenues for practical interventions designed to balance online discourse and promote exposure to diverse viewpoints, which could help temper the polarizing effects of confirmation bias.

In conclusion, this study contributes valuable insights that advance theoretical discourse, offer practical applications, and fill a critical gap in the literature. By exploring the dual impacts of content creation and temporal dynamics on confirmation bias, particularly in the context of social movements, this research guides the next steps in fostering positive social change. This suggests that digital platforms, educators, and content creators might use these findings to enhance content moderation and design practices in ways that encourage open-minded engagement from diverse perspectives. This study's combination of passive and active engagement methods offers a model for understanding the complex interplay between cognitive bias and digital environments in the age of information, providing a roadmap for mitigating the potentially adverse effects of confirmation bias in contemporary media landscapes.

The findings of this study contribute to a deeper understanding of how confirmation bias operates in digital environments, providing a foundation for developing interventions to reduce its impact on information consumption and dissemination behaviours. By investigating how individuals search for, engage with, and recall information in real-world contexts such as the Black Lives Matter (BLM) movement, this study reveals the persistent nature of preexisting attitudes and the extent to which these attitudes shape digital interactions. The introduction of the

Thinking-Absorption-Reinforcement-Time (TART) model provides a structured lens through which to examine these behaviours and offers a pathway for future research to explore cognitive biases within the complexities of the digital age. Insights from this study are essential in informing strategies aimed at fostering open-mindedness and promoting critical thinking in an increasingly polarized information landscape.

Expanding the main study to include a larger participant pool (N = 80) enabled a more comprehensive examination of the dynamics between memory retrieval and confirmation bias within a simulated online environment. The pilot study served as a preliminary investigation, while the main study incorporated modifications that enhanced the study's ecological validity. For example, the experimental manipulation in the main study involved content creation through simulated tweets, providing a platform that more closely resembles the nature of digital discourse. Both groups in the main study were also prompted with a memory task: the control group responded to multiple-choice questions, whereas the experimental group generated a tweet.

These methodological distinctions allowed the study to explore more nuanced aspects of engagement, particularly the hypothesis that active engagement, such as content creation, would intensify confirmation bias compared with passive engagement. While both groups exhibited confirmation bias, the feedback loop fostered through active engagement appeared to accelerate confirmation-seeking behaviour during digital news consumption. This insight aligns with the broader theory that active engagement in content creation strengthens the cognitive processes that reinforce preexisting beliefs.

Three sub-hypotheses were also examined to parse the effects of content engagement modes on confirmation bias:

- Sub-Hypothesis 1: Active content consumption, involving tasks such as content creation, is hypothesized to heighten confirmation bias due to increased engagement with the material. The findings indicated that the experimental group exhibited a more pronounced shift towards confirmatory information search, particularly in the initial level of opinion polarization (Pol_pre) and subsequent attitude change (AoC). This suggests that active engagement amplifies confirmation bias by facilitating a deeper interaction with material aligned with existing views.

- Sub-Hypothesis 2: Passive content consumption, defined by reading and answering multiple-choice questions, was expected to reinforce confirmation bias by allowing participants to consume content without the interactive layer that might challenge established beliefs. The study supported this hypothesis by demonstrating that participants with strongly polarized initial attitudes showed less change, reinforcing the notion that passive consumption limits the potential for belief modification.

- Sub-Hypothesis 3: The moderating role of temporal delay and content source credibility was explored as a potential factor in the relationship between the engagement mode and confirmation bias. The findings suggest that temporal delays and source disclosure influence confirmation bias intensity, underscoring the complex interplay between initial opinions, engagement modes, and perceived source credibility. Both groups exhibited confirmation bias, yet the experimental group reached confirmatory search levels faster than the control group did, suggesting that active engagement without a temporal delay accelerated confirmatory behaviour.

This combined analysis reinforces the conclusion that content engagement and temporal dynamics play distinct roles in shaping confirmation bias. The experimental group's rapid shift towards confirmatory behaviour highlights the potential for active content creation to expedite the feedback loop of confirmation-seeking behaviour in digital environments. This convergence of results across studies supports the notion that the reinforcement of confirmation bias can be accelerated through engagement in content creation.

The integration of findings from both studies presents a more holistic view of confirmation bias in media consumption, specifically within the context of the BLM movement. The key differences between the pilot and main study results illustrate how the type of engagement affects attitude reinforcement and change:

- Pilot study: Both groups exhibited minimal attitude changes, with the experimental group showing a slight decrease from 6.25 to 5.95 and the control group decreasing from 7.3 to 6.65. These shifts were minor, suggesting a limited impact of the intervention at this stage.
- Main study: The expanded participant pool and engagement with content creation tasks in the main study revealed slightly different patterns. The experimental group presented a slight increase in BLM scale scores (+0.07), whereas the control group presented a slight decrease (−0.025), indicating that active engagement may prompt more noticeable changes in bias intensity over time.

The study's findings highlight the inherent complexity of modifying attitudes through media interaction alone. Simply increasing exposure to diverse viewpoints or enhancing the depth of engagement may not suffice to meaningfully shift strongly held beliefs, particularly in polarized contexts. Both groups in the main study consistently selected news articles aligned with their preexisting beliefs, indicating strong confirmation bias across modes of engagement. The persistence of confirmation bias in both experimental conditions underscores the need for media literacy strategies that move beyond exposure and encourage critical reflection on one's own biases.

The findings of this research illuminate the intricate dynamics of memory recall, selective exposure, and content creation in shaping confirmation bias. Across both the pilot and main studies, the results indicated that individuals with strong initial opinions on contentious issues such as the BLM movement were less likely to modify their attitudes, even when engaging in active content creation. Notably, participants with less extreme initial views demonstrated greater receptivity to change, suggesting that the degree of initial polarization plays a critical role in the reinforcement or modification of biases.

The main study findings further demonstrated that active engagement through content creation accelerated the shift towards confirmatory search behaviour compared with passive engagement. The participants who engaged in content creation moved towards confirmatory information at a faster rate, supporting the hypothesis that active engagement intensifies confirmation bias by reinforcing selective exposure patterns.

Additionally, the study revealed that temporal dynamics and the engagement mode influence the speed and strength of bias reinforcement, highlighting the complex interplay between how content is consumed and the reinforcement of preexisting beliefs.

By examining confirmation bias within digital environments, this study underscores the importance of fostering media literacy practices that encourage self-awareness and balanced information consumption.

Analysing the data from both the experimental and control groups offers nuanced insights into how preexisting attitudes and content engagement influence opinion shifts on topics such as the BLM movement. The study's primary hypothesis posited that the content consumption mode would affect confirmation bias intensity, shaped by initial polarization and engagement type. The study's findings supported this hypothesis, demonstrating that the content engagement mode affects bias reinforcement, although confirmation bias persisted across both active and passive consumption modes.

- Confirmation Bias Intensity and Engagement Mode: Active content consumption—specifically content creation—was linked to stronger confirmation bias, reflected in more confirmatory news selections and greater resistance to attitude change. The experimental group showed a moderate negative correlation ($r = -0.53$) between initial polarization and attitude change, highlighting that those who engaged in content creation exhibited stronger confirmation-seeking behaviour.
- Patterns of News Selection: Both groups, regardless of engagement mode, exhibited a preference for confirmatory news, illustrating the persistence of confirmation bias across different content consumption methods. This suggests that even active engagement does not inherently reduce confirmation bias, underscoring the challenge of disrupting entrenched biases.

The study's findings suggest that while active engagement can influence the intensity of confirmation bias, it does not necessarily mitigate it. This pattern reveals the complexity of designing interventions to combat confirmation bias within digital media contexts. For example, the consistency in confirmatory news selection across both groups suggests that interventions should address not only content exposure but also strategies to promote reflection on initial attitudes.

The TART model introduced in this study—encompassing the Thinking, Absorption, Reinforcement, and Time phases—aligns closely with the observed behaviours in the main study. Each phase corresponds with specific behaviours and cognitive processes identified in the research:

1. Thinking phase: During this initial phase, individuals gravitate towards information that confirms their preexisting beliefs. This tendency was evident in the study's observation of confirmatory search patterns, where participants selected headlines aligning with their views.
2. Absorption phase: In this phase, individuals internalize information that resonates with their biases. The research indicated that both the passive and active engagement modes led to the internalization of confirmatory content, supporting the entrenchment of biases.
3. Reinforcement phase: Active engagement through content creation heightened this phase, as participants' direct interaction with content reinforced their confirmation biases.
4. Time phase: Temporal dynamics further affected confirmation bias, with the control group experiencing a delay in confirmatory search compared with the experimental group. This phase underscores the potential impact of temporal delays on bias reinforcement.

The alignment of the TART model with this study underscores its utility in understanding the sequential process of bias reinforcement in digital environments.

5.2   Discussion of Limitations, Validity Threats, and Recommendations for Future Research

While this study offers important insights into confirmation bias, selective exposure, and the broader dynamics of digital information processing, several limitations and validity considerations need to be addressed. These considerations relate to the generalizability of the findings (external validity), the reliability of the study design (internal validity), and the alignment between theoretical constructs and practical measurement (construct validity). Each of these aspects is discussed in detail below.

Ensuring external validity, or the extent to which findings can be generalized beyond the specific context of the study, was a primary consideration. To enhance this generalizability, participants, such as university students or a local sample, were recruited from Amazon's Mechanical Turk rather than from a more homogeneous population. This approach allowed for a demographically diverse participant pool, capturing a range of ages, backgrounds, and perspectives. The choice to use Mechanical Turk facilitated a sample that better represents a broad spectrum of the general population, thus increasing the study's external validity.

The study environment was meticulously tailored to reflect real-world online information consumption as closely as possible. The participants interacted with a custom-designed digital platform that aimed to simulate a typical online content browsing and creation experience. This environment allowed for a level of ecological validity that might be lacking in more traditional lab-based studies. It also mitigated some of the reactivity concerns often associated with experimental setups, as participants were not informed of the study's true purpose until completion, reducing potential self-censorship or behaviour modification aimed at pleasing the researchers.

Despite these strategies, certain aspects of the study's design may still limit the generalizability of the findings. For example, while Mechanical Turk provides access to a diverse sample, it does have its own biases: participants on the platform are more likely to be experienced in completing online tasks, which could influence their interactions with the study environment. Additionally, the global nature of online information exposure means that digital media consumption patterns can vary widely by culture, region, and social context. Thus, while the study's design minimizes some external validity threats, the findings might still be more representative of Western digital media users than a truly global population.

Furthermore, external factors such as participants' immediate environment or prior exposure to related topics could also influence the study's outcomes. Participants' responses might be affected by the setting in which they completed the study (such as a quiet room versus a public space), as well as by any recent exposure to similar content on social media, potentially influencing their levels of bias or polarization. While it is challenging to control for such variables in online studies, future research could attempt to measure or account for these environmental factors to further strengthen external validity.

In summary, while this study has made deliberate efforts to enhance generalizability through sample diversity and a realistic digital environment, some uncontrollable external factors may still influence the generalizability of the findings. Despite these limitations, however, the study's results offer valuable insights into the dynamics of confirmation bias and selective exposure, which are likely relevant across diverse online contexts.

Internal validity, or the extent to which the study design accurately isolates the relationship between the variables and outcomes, was another primary focus. Given that the study was designed to examine causal relationships—particularly between types of content engagement (active versus passive) and the reinforcement of confirmation bias—it was crucial to minimize potential internal validity threats.

One common threat to internal validity is the influence of history effects, where external events occurring during the study period might impact participants' responses. To mitigate this risk, the study was conducted within a tightly controlled timeframe, minimizing the likelihood that unrelated external events could impact participants' responses. However, given the dynamic nature of current events, particularly around a topic as relevant as Black Lives Matter, it remains possible that participants were influenced by recent news or media exposure related to social justice issues.

Another concern is maturation, where changes in participants' psychological or physical states over time could influence the results. In this case, the relatively short duration of the study helps mitigate this risk, as there was limited opportunity for significant personal changes to occur. Additionally, the diverse demographic profile of the participant pool further reduces the likelihood of maturation effects affecting all participants in the same way.

To address potential issues of statistical regression—where extreme initial scores tend to gravitate towards the mean in subsequent measurements—control groups were used alongside pre-test measures. This approach allowed for clearer distinctions between genuine treatment effects and statistical artifacts. By incorporating control groups and pre-tests, the study was able to observe more accurately how different content engagement modes influenced confirmation bias. These measures help establish a stronger basis for interpreting causality within the study's hypotheses.

Randomization of participants and careful design of experimental conditions were also implemented to safeguard against selection bias and other internal validity threats. For example, participants were randomly assigned to either active or passive content engagement conditions, minimizing the risk of self-selection effects that might otherwise skew the results. Randomization, combined with a clear structure for data collection and control over conditions, helped ensure that any observed differences in confirmation bias could be attributed to the nature of content engagement rather than extraneous variables.

A final consideration related to internal validity is the potential impact of participant expectations or demand characteristics—where participants' awareness of the study's objectives might influence their responses. Although the true purpose of the study was masked until completion, subtle cues or prior experience with similar studies could still influence behaviour. This limitation is inherent to studies where participants are aware of being observed, even in online settings, and is especially relevant in studies related to sensitive or polarizing topics. In the future, further masking of study intent and follow-up debriefs might help clarify whether demand characteristics influence results.

In conclusion, through meticulous design, randomization, and control mechanisms, this study has made strong efforts to protect internal validity. However, certain uncontrollable factors, such as participants' prior knowledge or assumptions about the study, may still have had some impact on the outcomes. Nonetheless, the measures taken provide a solid foundation for the validity of the causal inferences drawn from this research.

Construct validity concerns the alignment between the theoretical concepts being studied and the actual measures or procedures used to represent these concepts in the research. In this study, ensuring construct validity was essential, as key constructs such as confirmation bias, selective exposure, and attitude change are complex and multifaceted.

To strengthen construct validity, validated measurement tools and a comprehensive pilot study were employed to refine the procedures and confirm that the methods effectively captured the intended constructs. For example, attitudes towards the Black Lives Matter movement were assessed via a Likert scale, which allowed for nuanced measurement of participants' views across a spectrum, providing insight into the level of polarization and enabling a quantifiable measure of attitude change. The choice of a Likert scale, a commonly accepted measure in psychology research, was intended to capture subtle shifts in participant attitudes accurately.

One specific threat to construct validity in this study is the potential for measurement validity issues. In this context, measurement validity refers to whether the tools used (e.g. Likert scales and news selection metrics) effectively capture the nuances of confirmation bias and attitude polarization. If these measures fail to capture subtle aspects of these constructs or if participants misinterpret the scales or selection tasks, then the findings might not fully represent the phenomena under study. To address this, we utilized validated scales and piloted the study with a smaller group to test for any ambiguities in the measures.

Another challenge to construct validity lies in the sensitivity of the study topic, which could lead to social desirability bias. Given that participants were asked about attitudes towards a highly polarizing issue, some may have felt compelled to respond in ways they believed were socially acceptable rather than honestly reflecting their views. Social desirability bias can cause discrepancies between reported opinions and actual attitudes, particularly in studies addressing sensitive topics. To mitigate this, participants were assured of anonymity and confidentiality, reducing the likelihood of biased responses and encouraging more genuine answers.

Demand characteristics, where participants alter their responses on the basis of what they perceive the researchers expect, also present a potential threat to construct validity. Participants who believe that they understand the study's purpose may subconsciously adjust their behaviour to align with perceived expectations. To reduce this risk, a cover story was used, concealing the study's primary focus on confirmation bias and selective exposure. This approach was intended to prevent participants from altering their behaviour to align with presumed research goals. Additionally, participants were debriefed at the end of the study, allowing for a clarification of the study's purpose, which may further minimize residual biases in their responses.

Finally, potential issues with construct validity may also arise from the operationalization of "active" versus "passive" engagement. In this study, active engagement was defined as participants creating content (e.g. writing tweets) in response to information, whereas passive engagement involved multiple-choice responses with limited personal input. While these distinctions were carefully designed to reflect different levels of engagement, participants may have perceived these tasks differently than anticipated. This issue, while challenging to eliminate entirely, was addressed by defining tasks as clearly as possible during the study introduction.

In summary, a range of measures were employed to enhance construct validity, from piloting and refining measurement tools to implementing strategies that minimize social desirability bias and demand characteristics. However, as with any study involving complex psychological constructs, a degree of interpretation is always involved in translating theory into measurable constructs, and future research might benefit from further refinement of these measures.

Ethical considerations are crucial aspects of any study, particularly one examining sensitive issues such as polarization and confirmation bias around social movements. Adhering to ethical guidelines and protecting participants' rights were paramount in the study's design and execution. This study was conducted in full compliance with the University of Nicosia's Ethics Committee, which provided oversight and approved the research protocol. The protocol included assessments of data protection, participant rights, and risk management to safeguard participant welfare and maintain procedural validity.

To ensure informed consent, all participants received a detailed information sheet outlining the study's purpose, procedures, and rights, including the right to withdraw at any time. This consent process was designed to be comprehensive, with clear language to ensure that participants understood what their involvement was. Additionally, anonymity was protected by using anonymized identification numbers on Mechanical Turk, ensuring that personal data were not processed or stored, thus maintaining participant confidentiality throughout the study.

The study also implemented robust data protection measures, storing anonymized data securely on password-protected computers and external hard drives. Only de-identified data were used for analysis, further ensuring participant privacy and data security. The participants were also assured that the data would only be accessible to the research team and that their identities could not be linked back to their responses.

Furthermore, to mitigate potential distress arising from the study's sensitive topics, participants were informed that they could withdraw at any point. Debriefing followed the study, during which participants were provided with information about the research's aims, any misconceptions clarified, and resources offered for further questions or concerns. This debriefing process ensured that participants left the study with a full understanding of their contribution and with no residual misunderstandings.

While ethical procedures were adhered to rigorously, it is important to acknowledge that, as in any online study, researchers had limited control over the participants' actual environments. Although the Mechanical Turk platform allowed for a diverse sample, the online nature of the study meant that the environment in which participants engaged could vary greatly, potentially influencing their responses. This limitation, while difficult to control, was mitigated as much as possible through clear instructions and a standardized study environment.

In conclusion, this study took extensive measures to maintain ethical standards, protect participants' privacy, and ensure that their rights were respected. The procedural validity of these efforts supports the reliability of the findings, as participants were able to engage with the study material freely, without coercion or undue influence. Nonetheless, ongoing advancements in ethical practices for online research, particularly regarding privacy and consent, will continue to shape future studies in this field.

To build on the findings of this study, future research should take a more comprehensive and nuanced approach in exploring how confirmation bias, selective exposure, and opinion polarization evolve over time, particularly within the fast-paced and polarized digital landscape. Below are several recommendations for future research directions that could further illuminate the intricate dynamics of cognitive biases in digital environments and provide deeper insights into how individuals process information and form opinions.

One of the most promising avenues for future research involves adopting a longitudinal design to examine the long-term effects of information exposure on individuals' opinions and behaviours. While the current study provided valuable insights through a cross-sectional approach, observing participants over an extended period would offer a more comprehensive view of how cognitive biases evolve and become reinforced or mitigated over time. Tracking individuals' opinion changes in real-world settings—ideally over months or even years—would allow researchers to explore questions such as the following:

- How stable are individuals' biases and polarized beliefs over time?
- What role does repeated exposure to like-minded versus contrasting content play in reinforcing or shifting these beliefs?
- Can certain interventions lead to gradual attitude shifts rather than immediate changes?

Longitudinal research would allow researchers to explore how confirmation bias interacts with life events, shifts in personal circumstances, or broader social influences, providing a more in-depth understanding of the persistence or malleability of cognitive bias. Additionally, by mapping how exposure to diverse or confirmatory information impacts individuals over time, this approach contributes valuable insights into the long-term efficacy of media literacy programmes and interventions aimed at promoting critical thinking and open-mindedness.

Another significant recommendation is to integrate future studies within actual social media environments. Conducting research within real platforms would provide a more authentic context for observing how opinions evolve and how confirmation bias operates in genuine online networks. Social media platforms such as Twitter, Facebook, and Instagram are rich in interactive elements—such as comments, shares, and likes—that are not easily replicated in controlled environments. By embedding studies in these spaces, researchers can observe the following:

- How participants' opinions shift in response to different types of engagement (e.g. comments from like-minded individuals versus dissenting opinions).
- The role of social reinforcement, such as likes or shares, is to strengthen individuals' biases and encourage them to seek out similar content.
- How interactions within echo chambers influence selective exposure and the extent of polarized opinion formation.

Social media-based research could also focus on the algorithms that drive content exposure, examining how automated recommendations reinforce or challenge participants' views. Tracking users' interactions on these platforms could reveal important data on the reinforcement of biases through online social validation and content algorithms. Although privacy and ethical considerations present obstacles, with proper anonymization, informed consent, and compliance with data privacy laws, this form of research could yield invaluable insights into the mechanisms of confirmation bias in the digital age.

The application of dynamic modelling techniques, such as agent-based models and temporal modelling, would provide a deeper understanding of how confirmation bias unfolds over time and across various conditions. Dynamic models can simulate temporal patterns of opinion change, helping researchers predict how individuals' biases may shift on the basis of different types of information exposure, engagement, or social feedback. For instance:

- Agent-based models can simulate interactions between individuals within digital spaces, modelling how selective exposure and reinforcement from like-minded individuals lead to the formation of echo chambers.
- Temporal modelling could allow for detailed tracking of attitude change over time, showing how biases emerge, strengthen, or even wane as participants repeatedly engage with different types of content.

These techniques enable researchers to observe how cognitive biases interact with variables such as the type of content, the time between exposures, and the influence of peer feedback. Through simulations and dynamic models, future research could develop a clearer picture of the feedback loops that drive selective exposure and opinion polarization.

A promising yet challenging direction for future research involves real-time monitoring of user behaviour to capture participants' interactions and cognitive processes as they engage with digital content. Real-time data could include users' search behaviours, click patterns, and immediate responses to new information. This would provide an authentic view of how confirmation bias influences information processing in real time. Some potential areas to explore through real-time monitoring include the following:

- How users' initial search queries and click patterns reflect their biases and potentially lead to selective exposure from the outset.
- The extent to which users selectively avoid information that challenges their views, particularly when they have immediate access to confirmatory content.
- The interaction between content type (e.g. sensational vs. factual headlines) and users' propensity to engage with or avoid certain information.

Despite the privacy concerns and ethical barriers that such an approach may present, with proper protocols and anonymization, real-time monitoring could significantly advance our understanding of confirmation bias as a moment-to-moment phenomenon. However, owing to the complexity of implementing this type of study ethically, future research may need to rely on experimental simulations that approximate real-time monitoring conditions while protecting participants' privacy.

Given the globalization of information and digital media, exploring cognitive biases and selective exposure across diverse cultural contexts would provide valuable insights into how different societal values and norms shape the manifestation of confirmation bias. The cultural context can greatly influence information-seeking behaviours, with individuals in different societies potentially showing varied preferences for confirmatory versus challenging content. Future cross-cultural studies could explore the following questions:

- Do individualistic cultures show a greater tendency towards selective exposure than collectivistic cultures do, where community and social harmony may discourage polarized viewpoints?
- How do cultural attitudes towards authority, collectivism, and openness to new information impact confirmation bias in digital spaces?
- Are certain types of bias (e.g. confirmation bias vs. status quo bias) more pronounced in particular cultural settings?

By examining how confirmation bias and selective exposure manifest across diverse societies, future research could help tailor interventions and educational initiatives to different cultural contexts, potentially leading to more effective methods for reducing polarization and encouraging open-minded engagement with information.

Another key recommendation for future research is to study how individuals navigate information across multiple platforms, such as social media, news websites, podcasts, and video content. Today's media landscape is highly fragmented, with people accessing information from an array of sources, each with its own presentation style and degree of interactivity. Analysing participants' behaviour across platforms could shed light on how different content types and presentation formats influence confirmation bias and selective exposure. Specific areas for investigation might include the following:

- How does the format and design of each platform influence users' information-seeking behaviours (e.g. scrolling, clicking, liking, commenting)?
- Whether individuals exhibit consistent confirmation bias across platforms or if certain platforms amplify or mitigate bias differently.
- How engagement with a particular platform, such as the more passive consumption of news articles versus the active engagement required by social media, affects opinion formation and bias reinforcement.

By examining behaviours across platforms, future research can develop a more holistic view of how individuals' information processing is shaped in the digital age and identify potential platform-specific interventions that reduce confirmation bias.

The role of source credibility and news framing in confirmation bias also warrants further research. People are increasingly aware of media bias and the reputation of information sources, which can influence their willingness to accept or reject information. Investigating how perceptions of source credibility affect selective exposure and opinion polarization would provide insights into the following:

- Whether higher perceived credibility of a source reduces the likelihood of selective exposure and encourages more balanced engagement with content.
- How framing, such as sensational versus factual tones, affects the reinforcement of biases and selective exposure across various demographic groups.
- The relationship between political orientation and perceptions of source credibility involves examining whether individuals tend to favour information sources that align with their ideological beliefs.

By exploring these questions, future research could inform strategies that help users evaluate information sources more critically, potentially reducing the influence of selective exposure and confirmation bias.

Future studies would also benefit from integrating cognitive and emotional factors into the analysis of confirmation bias. For example, cognitive load can impact individuals' willingness to engage with challenging information, as a high cognitive load may lead individuals to favour simpler, confirmatory information. Emotional responses, such as anxiety, anger, or excitement, can also impact information selection and retention. Future research might explore the following:

- How emotional responses to content impact selective exposure, with a focus on whether strong emotional reactions (e.g. outrage or joy) drive individuals towards confirmatory or sensational information.
- The influence of cognitive load on selective exposure, testing whether lower cognitive load conditions reduce confirmation bias by enabling greater engagement with complex or challenging content.
- The effect of self-reflection prompts before information exposure to reduce bias by encouraging a mindset of openness and curiosity.

Examining the cognitive and emotional dimensions would provide a more comprehensive understanding of the internal factors that drive confirmation bias, adding depth to models of cognitive processing in digital contexts.

Given the persistence of confirmation bias across both active and passive content consumption, as observed in this study, future research should test interventions that encourage critical thinking and self-reflection in digital interactions. Potential interventions to explore include the following:

- **Content flags or nudges**: Implementing flags that encourage users to consider alternative perspectives or engage critically with content before engaging.
- **Reflexive tasks**: Prompting users to write about their assumptions before reading content, with the goal of fostering a mindset of critical reflection.
- **Balanced information exposure**: Experiments with algorithms that expose users to diverse viewpoints within a structured environment to determine whether this approach mitigates bias over time.

Such interventions could be tested in controlled environments or through collaborations with digital platforms, offering insights into practical strategies that foster balanced perspectives and reduce polarization.

By leveraging these future research directions, studies can expand on the foundational insights gained from this investigation into confirmation bias, selective exposure, and opinion polarization in digital environments. By adopting longitudinal approaches, engaging real-world social media environments, incorporating multiplatform analysis, and testing interventions, researchers can build a more nuanced understanding of how digital interactions shape individual beliefs over time. These advancements promise to offer a richer comprehension of confirmation bias within the broader social and cognitive landscape, ultimately contributing to efforts that foster critical thinking, open-mindedness, and balanced perspectives in the digital age.

5.3 Strategies to Mitigate the Impact of Confirmation Bias on Digital Platforms, Including Educational and Policy-Based Interventions

Burton (2023) emphasized the importance of redefining AI security frameworks to account more effectively for their impact on human behaviour and social dynamics. The crux of our study elucidates the intricate interplay between confirmation bias and digital information consumption. Using the TART (Thinking-Absorption-Reinforcement-Time) model as a framework, the research illuminates the progression through phases of bias-seeking, passive absorption, active reinforcement, and temporal dynamics. This model reveals two pivotal insights. First, active engagement, such as content creation and commentary, amplifies existing biases, aligning with the reinforcement phase of the TART model. Second, temporal dynamics—such as the timing of memory retrieval influenced by content creation—might further intensify biases. As digital platforms shape public opinion and discourse, the challenge lies in designing strategies that address these mechanisms to encourage balanced perspectives and reduce polarization.

To address confirmation bias effectively on digital platforms, strategies must incorporate both educational and policy-based interventions. These measures can empower individuals to engage more critically with information, foster exposure to diverse viewpoints, and help platforms design algorithms that do not inadvertently reinforce bias. Below, we explore how educational approaches and policy-driven initiatives can work together to reduce the impact of confirmation bias.

Promoting Digital Literacy and Critical Thinking

Digital literacy programmes such as Norway's Tenk initiative are essential for equipping individuals with the skills needed to navigate the complexities of today's digital landscape. Established in 2019, Tenk focused on bridging gaps in the Norwegian educational system by fostering media and information literacy among young people. By teaching critical assessment of information, Tenk has successfully empowered its participants to engage thoughtfully with digital content and tools (Tenk, n.d.). However, similar initiatives are not widely implemented in other regions, largely due to several systemic challenges.

One of the primary barriers to broader adoption is resource limitations. Many educational institutions, particularly those in underserved areas, lack the infrastructure, tools, and funding required to implement digital literacy programmes. Without access to modern computer labs, up-to-date software, or reliable Internet connections, the integration of such initiatives becomes nearly impossible (Futurize Studio, n.d.). Additionally, existing school curricula often leave little room for incorporating digital literacy. With packed schedules and pressure to meet standardized testing requirements, educators face difficulties in allocating time for new subjects, regardless of their degree of vitality (Meridha, 2024).

Another significant challenge is the need for adequately trained teachers. Digital literacy education relies on educators who are proficient in using digital tools and technologies. Unfortunately, many teachers lack this training, creating a skills gap that undermines efforts to implement these programmes effectively (Meridha, 2024). In addition to technical barriers, cultural attitudes also play a role. In some regions, there is scepticism about the value of digital literacy or resistance to adopting new educational approaches, further slowing progress (Meridha, 2024).

Overcoming these obstacles requires coordinated efforts, including targeted investments in infrastructure, robust teacher training programmes, and the integration of digital literacy into national education policies. The success of initiatives such as Tenk demonstrates that these efforts are not only possible but also profoundly impactful. By learning from the Nordic model, countries around the world can build programmes that empower their populations with the critical skills necessary to thrive in an increasingly digital world.

Educational interventions form the backbone of strategies to mitigate confirmation bias. Digital literacy programmes that emphasize critical thinking can equip users with the skills to evaluate information and resist the pull of confirmatory content. By fostering a better understanding of how biases shape perceptions and choices, digital literacy training can cultivate more informed media consumers.

Integrating media literacy into formal education can be a powerful tool for helping individuals understand and counteract cognitive biases, particularly confirmation bias, selective exposure, and echo chambers. By incorporating media literacy courses into school curricula, educators can provide students with a foundational awareness of how biases shape information processing and how digital algorithms often amplify these biases. Lessons that use real-world examples from social media, news outlets, and search engines can make these concepts tangible, illustrating the mechanisms behind biased information consumption.

In addition to theoretical understanding, fostering reflective thinking through case studies of real-world events affected by confirmation bias can help students recognize the pitfalls of selective information processing. By analysing instances where misinformation spreads widely due to confirmation bias, students learn to identify similar patterns in their information intake. Encouraging reflection on both personal biases and those inherent in information sources can prompt a more questioning, cautious approach to digital content.

The development of interactive learning tools, such as simulations and digital games, adds another dimension to media literacy education by engaging students in experiential learning. Through these tools, users can explore scenarios where confirmation bias influences outcomes, experiencing first-hand how echo chambers and selective exposure shape opinions over time. By simulating the formation of information bubbles, these tools foster critical engagement, helping users build a more sceptical, informed approach to navigating digital spaces.

Encouraging Diverse Perspectives in Digital Spaces

A central component of addressing confirmation bias on digital platforms is fostering exposure to a broader range of perspectives. In digital environments where algorithms prioritize content aligned with users' prior interactions, exposure to contrasting viewpoints is often limited. Strategies to ensure balanced exposure are crucial for mitigating echo chambers and promoting well-rounded understanding.

One approach to countering confirmation bias on social media platforms and search engines is through algorithmic adjustments that promote diverse content curation. Rather than exclusively showing users content that aligns with their preferences, algorithms can be designed to periodically introduce content from differing perspectives. Personalized content curation systems could balance user preferences with intentional diversity, helping to expose users to a wider range of viewpoints. While implementing such algorithms presents technical and user experience challenges, this strategy could reduce the reinforcement of biases without feeling intrusive to users.

The incorporation of "perspective broadening" features on platforms could further encourage users to explore diverse viewpoints. For example, when a user reads an article or post, the platform might suggest links to other articles that present alternative or contrasting perspectives. This subtle nudge encourages users to venture beyond their usual information bubbles. Platforms could also offer "perspective summaries" that distil differing viewpoints on contentious topics, giving users a broader view of the issues at a glance.

Promoting community dialogue and deliberation can also help miti-gate confirmation bias by facilitating constructive exchanges among users with diverse perspectives. Structured dialogues, moderated to prevent hostility and encourage respectful engagement, allow users to interact with differing opinions in a setting that fosters empathy and understand-ing. Platforms could further support this by incorporating prompts that emphasize the importance of open-mindedness, reminding users of the value of engaging with diverse thoughts and experiences.

Policy-Based Interventions to Promote Balanced Information

In addition to educational and platform-based strategies, policy interven-tions can play a significant role in addressing confirmation bias on digital platforms. Policies can help ensure that digital spaces prioritize accurate and balanced information dissemination. The following policy measures could be instrumental in this endeavour.

Establishing guidelines for responsible algorithm design can help digi-tal platforms mitigate the reinforcement of biases in content curation. Regulatory bodies could encourage platforms to integrate bias-reducing mechanisms within their algorithms, promoting transparency around how content is prioritized and recommended. Such guidelines might require platforms to disclose when content recommendations are based on prior user engagement, helping users recognize potential biases in their information consumption. By making the curation process more transparent, platforms can foster a more informed and balanced digital experience for users.

Encouraging regular algorithmic audits and accountability measures is another approach to ensuring responsible content management. Independent audits, conducted by third-party organizations, could assess whether platforms disproportionately amplify certain content, thereby creating echo chambers or reinforcing biases. The results of these audits should be publicly available, providing stakeholders with insight into a platform's commitment to balanced information ecosystems.

Accountability through such audits could push platforms to adopt practices that reduce the potential for biased content amplification.

Supporting fact-checking initiatives and implementing credibility indicators on platforms can further combat the influence of confirmation bias. By associating news articles and social media posts with credibility markers that denote source reliability, platforms can help users make more informed judgements about the content they encounter. This visual reinforcement encourages critical assessment, helps users navigate information more thoughtfully and reduces the likelihood of confirmation bias fuelled by misinformation.

Raising Awareness of Cognitive Biases and Encouraging Self-Reflection

Effective mitigation of confirmation bias requires individuals to become more self-aware and reflective about their information consumption patterns. Educational programmes and digital tools that encourage self-reflection can prompt users to critically examine their beliefs and biases, fostering a mindset conducive to balanced information processing.

The development of self-assessment tools for bias awareness can empower users to recognize the influences shaping their digital interactions. By answering questions about their beliefs, values, and preferred information sources, users gain insights into the biases that may impact their information consumption. These tools could suggest personalized strategies for mitigating bias, such as deliberately seeking diverse sources or exploring opposing viewpoints. In doing so, users become more conscious of the potential echo chambers they inhabit and more proactive in broadening their perspectives.

Integrating subtle nudges on digital platforms can further encourage users to reflect before sharing or commenting on content. For example, a platform might prompt users to "consider alternative perspectives" or remind them to verify information from multiple sources before sharing. These prompts foster mindful engagement and reduce impulsive actions driven by confirmation bias, helping users develop more deliberate and balanced approaches to interacting with content.

Educating users on the mechanics of the TART model—comprising Thinking, Absorption, Reinforcement, and Time—can also increase their awareness of how digital content reinforces biases over time. By understanding how each phase influences information processing and bias formation, users may adopt a more critical approach to how they consume and respond to digital content. This model encourages users to recognize and disrupt automatic bias-reinforcing cycles, fostering a more reflective and balanced digital experience.

Encouraging Responsible Content Creation and Sharing

As our research highlights, active content creation and sharing contribute significantly to confirmation bias reinforcement. To mitigate this, users need to be aware of the responsibilities associated with content creation and how sharing content can affect public discourse.

Promoting media literacy programmes focused on the impact of content creation can help users understand how sharing information contributes to confirmation bias within their networks. Educating users on how their content choices influence the biases of others encourages a more conscientious approach to sharing. Media literacy efforts can provide practical guidelines for assessing the credibility of sources and verifying information accuracy before sharing, empowering users to make responsible content choices.

The incorporation of content verification and fact-checking tools on platforms can further encourage responsible sharing. By providing built-in verification prompts, especially on contentious topics, platforms can integrate third-party fact-checking resources that urge users to verify claims before posting. This feature can help curb the spread of misinformation by fostering a culture of accountability among content creators and encouraging users to pause and verify before disseminating information.

Highlighting the role of content creation in echo chamber formation can also increase user awareness of the effects of selective sharing. When users predominantly share information that aligns with their existing views, they may inadvertently contribute to closed information loops that reinforce biases and limit exposure to diverse perspectives. By educating users on this phenomenon, platforms can promote a more balanced approach to sharing, fostering greater openness to varied viewpoints and a healthier digital information environment.

Empowering Users to Actively Seek Diverse Perspectives

To reduce confirmation bias, digital platforms can incorporate tools that enable users to explore a wider array of viewpoints actively.

Creating "Explore More" buttons that guide users to related content from differing perspectives can broaden users' information exposure on digital platforms. For example, after reading an article on a political topic, users could be encouraged to view opinions from various sides of the issue, actively exploring a range of viewpoints. This feature fosters a more balanced understanding by prompting users to seek diverse perspectives rather than remaining within a single ideological frame.

Curating "Challenge Your Beliefs" sections could further support this aim by providing content that intentionally contrasts with users' usual viewpoints. Algorithmically generated, these sections could offer balanced perspectives on popular issues, encouraging users to confront and consider alternative views. Such a feature would break the cycle of confirmation bias by actively introducing contrasting information, helping to create a more open and diverse information ecosystem.

Providing a tool to track information consumption diversity could also empower users to monitor their own content habits. By displaying the diversity of their content consumption—such as the percentage of content from varying perspectives—users can become more aware of their informational exposure. This awareness could inspire a more balanced approach to digital engagement, encouraging users to seek diverse sources and perspectives.

This book underscores the importance of addressing confirmation bias in digital spaces, especially given its reinforcement through active and passive engagement patterns. By implementing strategies that educate users, adjust algorithms, foster transparency, and encourage critical thinking, digital platforms can play a transformative role in fostering a balanced, less polarized information environment. As individuals become more cognizant of how confirmation bias shapes their digital interactions, a pathway opens towards more informed, constructive, and inclusive public discourse, supporting a healthier digital information ecosystem.

In addressing conspiracy theories, it is crucial to recognize that their appeal often stems from deeper psychological and social needs—such as the desire for certainty, control, and belonging—particularly in times of crisis or uncertainty. Combating these beliefs is not about silencing dissent but rather about fostering a culture where truth and critical inquiry are valued and accessible. By investing in education, rebuilding trust in institutions, leveraging technology responsibly, and encouraging open dialogue, we can create a resilient society that is less vulnerable to the allure of misinformation. While the challenge is ongoing, collective action across communities, governments, and organizations can help build a future where informed decision-making prevails over baseless speculation.

References

Bergerot, C., Barfuss, W., & Romanczuk, P. (2024). *Moderate confirmation bias enhances collective decision-making in reinforcement-learning agents.* bioRxiv 2023.2011. 2021.568073.

Burton, J. (2023). Algorithmic extremism? The securitization of artificial intelligence (AI) and its impact on radicalism, polarization and political violence. *Technology in Society, 75,* 102262. https://doi.org/10.1016/j. techsoc.2023.102262

Futurize Studio. (n.d., November 26). *What is digital literacy and its role in education?* https://www.futurize.studio/blog/what-is-digital-literacy-and-its-role-in-education

Meridha, J. M. (2024). The causes of poor digital literacy in educational practice, and possible solutions among the stakeholders: A systematic literature review. *SN Social Sciences, 4*(11), 210. https://doi.org/10.1007/s43545-024-01010-8

Tenk. (n.d., November 26). *About us*. https://tenk.faktisk.no/artikkel/about-us

Trang, S., Kraemer, T., Trenz, M., & Weiger, W. H. (2024). Deeper down the rabbit hole: How technology conspiracy beliefs emerge and foster a conspiracy mindset. *Information Systems Research*. https://doi.org/10.1287/isre.2022.0494

Index

The manufacturer's authorised representative in the EU is Springer
Nature Customer Service Centre GmbH, Europaplatz 3, 69115 Heidelberg,
Germany. If you have any concerns regarding our products, please
contact ProductSafety@springernature.com

Printed and bound by CPI Group (UK) Ltd, Croydon, CR0 4YY

29/04/2026

02099471-0013